WHY MOST POWERPOINT PRESENTATIONS SUCK

SUCK

And how you can make them better

Rick
Altman

www.betterppt.com

Why Most PowerPoint Presentations Suck

And how you can make them better

by Rick Altman

Published by:
Harvest Books
1423 Harvest Rd.
Pleasanton CA 94566
925.398.6210
www.betterppt.com

Library of Congress Control Number
2007924582

ISBN
978-0-6151-4223-4

Printed in the United States of America

To my four girls—beloved wife Becky, darling daughters Erica and Jamie, and loyal canine Missy. Once in a while, my household rank improves to fourth...

Contents

Foreword viii

Thanks To.... ix

Introduction x

Part One   **The Pain**

Chapter 1   **The 15-Minute Syndrome**   **3**
Who Are These People??. 4
Why Is This Happening? 5

Chapter 2   **The Cram-Everything-In Obsession**   **7**

Chapter 3   **Look at Me!!**   **11**

Chapter 4   **Bitter Backgrounds**   **15**
Backgrounds Shouldn't Be in the Foreground 16
Looking for Contrast in All the Wrong Places 17

Chapter 5   **The Scourge that is Custom Animation**   **19**
Your Audience is at Your Mercy 20
Your Covenant with the Audience. 21
How Much is Too Much?. 22

Chapter 6   **Can PowerPoint Make You Stupid?**   **25**
Where Good Ideas Go to Die 26
Talking Points Can Create Talking Heads 28
The Wrong Place to Start. 30

Part Two   **The Solution**

Chapter 7   **Surviving Bullets**   **37**
Three Words. 38
When the Words Must Display 41
The War Against "On Click" 42
Life is Too Short 44
The Art of Compromise 46

Chapter 8   **Be the Master of Your Own Slide**   **51**

A Semantic of Questions. 52
Understanding the Slide Master 53
Creating Multiple Masters. .55
Mixing and Matching. 58
Understanding Templates. .59
The New Horizon of Version 2007 60
Master Miscellany 64

Chapter 9   **Creating Custom Shows**   **65**

Many Shows, One File. 66
Less Flotsam, Better Focus. 67
Case Study. 67

Chapter 10   **The Art of Transparency**   **71**

Through the Looking Glass .72
Applying Transparency to Photos 76
Better Graphics with Version 2007 83
Raising Your Graphic IQ 84

Chapter 11   **Thriving with Animation**   **87**

Wisely and Appropriately 88
Three Steps to Better Animation. 91
A Word About Pace 93
Did PowerPoint Animation Win a Case? 101

Chapter 12   **More with Animation**   **105**

Two Animations, One Moment in Time. 106
Please Leave by the Exits. .110
The Path to Motion 113
Using the Advanced Timeline. 114
Be Conspicuous in Your Tastefulness 117

Part Three   Death, Taxes, and Public Speaking

Chapter 13   **Better than Bullets**   **121**
Communicating With Your Hands 122
Learning How to do Nothing 126

Chapter 14   **Fighting Nerves**   **131**
The Lowdown on Laughing 132
How Slow Can You Go? 133
Air Under the Pits 135

Chapter 15   **Working the Room**   **139**
Home Base 140
Going Out into the Deep End 141
Johnny, It's Time to Come Home... 143
Becoming One with Your Bullets 145
The Magical B Key 147
Mythbusting 148

Chapter 16   **Thoughts From The Experts**   **151**
Know Your Audience 152
Be Yourself 153
Guy Kawasaki 154
Being Prepared 155
TJ Walker 156
Storytelling 157
And Finally... 157

Part Four   Working Smarter, Presenting Better

Chapter 17   **Building a Better Interface**   **161**
Tool Terminology 101 162
Required Options 162
Flying Tools 167
Portable Icons 169
Your Personal Litmus Test 170
Optimizing Toolbar Space 172
Managing Your Personal Interface 175
Not Just a Question of Speed 175
Give Me Back My Interface! 176
The Downgrade that is Version 2007 178

Chapter 18   **Creating Intelligent Presentations**   **181**

Click Here, Go There 182
Hidden vs. Visible Hyperlinks 183
Flexible Intelligence 184
Hyperlinks Never Get Lost 185
Navigating Outside a Presentation 188
Using PowerPoint to Teach PowerPoint 192
Super- Geeky Tip No. 34B: Open Any File Like a Program 195
Creating Killer PowerPoint Menus 196
Trainer Heaven 202

Chapter 19   **Fabulous Photos**   **203**

Resolution Confusion 204
Welcome to the Better PPT Photo Lab 207
Managing the Move 211
Digital Photo Survival Skills 213

Chapter 20   **Music and Video: Looking Beyond PowerPoint**   **225**

Beyond Slides 226
Creating or Burning? 227
Please Insert Program Diskette 229
Making Memories, Evoking Emotions 230
Walking Through a Video Project 233
It's Your Music! 234
Our Toolbox 242

Chapter 21   **Junk & Miscellany**   **243**

Version 2007 244
Never Paste Again! 246
Heading Out the Door 247
Creating Self-Running Presentations 250
Start Me Up... 252
It's Midnight—Do You Know Where Your Templates Are? 253
Overheard at the PPT Newsgroup 255
Bringing Object Order to Chaos 258
Making Peace with Color Schemes 259
Dealing with Crappy Slides 261
And In the End... 267

Foreword

by Jim Endicott, Founder, Distinction Communication, Inc.

www.distinction-services.com

My morning routine starts with a 7:00 am trip to my favorite local drive-thru latte stand and I've found that in just 10 minutes, I can be back in my office checking emails with a hot beverage in hand. Recently my favorite spot went belly up so I drove a block further to another stand. "Double tall 20 oz. mocha - light on the chocolate," I requested. As far as lattes go, this order is pretty much a no-brainer so I was frustrated to find that it didn't taste at all like my usual drink.

At lunch I tried another stand and was frustrated with yet another version of a light chocolate mocha. The whole experience left me scratching my head. Everyone used pretty much the same ingredients but the results were dramatically different. So, what's up? Much like life, the real magic is in the hands of the craftsperson, not the tools they use.

For the most part, presenters today have access to all the same tools as well. They have a version of PowerPoint that isn't more than a few years old, an image editing program and maybe even a vector drawing application. But much like my latte experience, given the same basic ingredients, presenters and presentation designers manage somehow to produce dramatically different outcomes. One person using an older version of PowerPoint produces a masterful work of personal communication art while another using the latest software packages only manages to build a mind-numbing, convoluted, self-indulgent presentation that does little to accelerate information and ideas.

If audiences really are asking for more and we have a higher level of sensitivity to what doesn't work, why do so many still fail to deliver on those higher expectations? The answer is easy. Presenters and presentation designers still believe their presentations are all about them.

A reality check is in order. Audiences don't care about how much fun presenters are having with PowerPoint. Their collective brains go numb every time a presenter fills their screens with sub-sub-sub level bullets. Their use of animation is too often highly gratuitous and the pervasive stock flavor of everything on screen is a constant reminder their presentations have been brought to us courtesy of Microsoft wizards, not a single original thought.

All this being said, take heart, reader. There are those out there who are helping us better navigate the presentation design process and within these pages, Rick Altman helps shed some much needed light on this important business communication process. He challenges what's all too easy but also provides some much needed insight into what does work and how to do it. If you're like most presenters or presentation designers, you're looking for resources to help take your presentation visuals to the next essential level. Read on and begin to fill up your personal toolkit with the kinds of fresh insights and creative skills you can put to use in your next presentation.

Your audiences want more. It's time to finally deliver for them.

Thanks To... It might take a village to raise a child, and there are times when I feel a book cannot adequately be written without an entire community. I am fortunate to be part of a phenomenal one. The professional presentation community has many gathering points today, not the least of which is the PowerPoint Live User Conference, which I have hosted since 2003.

Each year, I have been privileged to have met some of the most passionate, enthusiastic, and dedicated presenters, designers, and content creators anywhere in the world. Their group energy is an almost intoxicating call to action for anyone who thinks out loud in public and I am tremendously grateful for having them in my head throughout this process.

And surprise, surprise, I don't have to venture past this group to assemble an excellent team of editors:

Chantal Bossé is a gifted trainer and presentations specialist from Quebec Canada. She was not only an eagle-eye through the text, but with English as her second language, she was a great reality check against some of my runaway jargon. She now knows what *bass-ackwards* means, so the relationship was of mutual benefit. **www.chabos.ca**

Kathy Jacobs is one of the legions of the Microsoft Most Valued Professional team of dedicated volunteers who help PowerPoint users with issues and questions. Her affinity for PowerPoint is so pronounced, when the Microsoft program developers attend PowerPoint Live, Kathy often supplies answers to development questions before they do. We also benefitted from the critical eye of Kathy's husband and techno wizard, Bruce. **www.onppt.com**

Sandra Johnson blends impeccable design sense, practical slide-making expertise, and fastidious attention to detail. In other words, she dinged me on bad-looking slides and misplaced periods—nothing that a bit of therapy won't solve... (Oh, and she doesn't like when I use ellipses.) **www.presentationwiz.biz**

I am also grateful to friend and illustrator **Paul Huntington** for help with the cover design. He says the vacuum cleaner was one of my better ideas, but as always, I relied on his keen eye and deft mouse hand to turn it into something great.

Introduction   The word he used was *meshuga,* known by both Jews and non-Jews alike to mean "crazy." And my father was looking right at me when he said it.

"You're going to say *that* in the book?"

"Actually, Dad, I'm going to say it in the title."

"You must be meshuga!"

And there you have either the most compelling reason to, or not to, author a book without the assist of a large publishing house. I've written for Sybex Books, Peachpit Press, Que Publishing, and several others, and I have the distinct impression that, were I to have followed that path this time, you would now be holding a book in your hands of a different name. Pretty good chance, as well, that a vacuum cleaner would not grace its cover.

My reason for choosing a private-label publisher was not because I sought an edgy title, although I do admit to enjoying the shock value that comes along for the ride. I did so because of a five-year-long frustration with being asked (make that required) to write on a clump of PowerPoint-centric topics that few in my intended audience find interesting.

Let's take a poll of one: Do you need to be taught how to create a slide? Did you buy this book because you don't understand how to make a string of text bold or how to make the bullet square instead of round?

If you bought this book for its intended purpose, it's because you have bigger issues.

- Your weekly load has now exceeded 200 slides and you are beginning to feel like a slide factory.

- Your presentations are not being received the way you were hoping they would and you're not sure why.

- You have good instincts but they need to be honed.

- Your co-worker keeps messing up your templates and you're about to scream.

- Your boss creates the most dismally-ugly slides and you don't know what to do about it.

- Or maybe...just maybe, it is you who needs a refresher in the principles of good presentation design.

Really, the potential market for this book is plenty vast without catering to the brand new user. How many horrible presentations did you sit through last month? In the face of how many colleagues or potential vendors would you like to stick this book and say "Here, please read this"?

I remember the first time I experienced it. I refer, of course, to the phenomenon we all know as Death by PowerPoint. The year was 1990, and three representatives from a well-known public relations firm wanted my partner and me to spend $10,000 on them to help us market a series of seminars.

They were smartly dressed, meticulously coiffed, and perfectly eloquent, as they proceeded to bore us out of our minds with drivel about value-added propositions, proactive initiatives, and positively-reinforced task-based personalization.

Every slide was read word for word, and each of us had a spiral-bound booklet that duplicated the slides.

Technically, this wasn't Death by PowerPoint; the software had not yet been invented. It was Death by Overhead Slide. Just as bad...

Who Should Read This Book?

As lead author, I would like to think that any presenter, presentation designer, or content creator would enjoy the pages of this book. The fact that I won't try to convince you of that is a sure sign that I have no future as a marketing consultant. From my annual conference and my on-going work as a presentations consultant and coach, I have a pretty good sense of the typical PowerPoint user. If I'm right, you fall into at least one of the following categories:

- You are thought of as the Slide King or Queen of your department and are called upon to crank out untold volumes of slides. Getting the job done on time becomes your sole focus.

- You are a presentation designer, where you have a bit more opportunity than the Slide King/Queen to consider the aesthetic side of content creation, but every project given to you is due yesterday.

- You are on the road a lot, giving sales presentations to audiences of various sizes. You have a well-worn template that fits you like a glove, never mind that it was designed from a wizard back in the 1990s. You have gotten pretty good at swapping in new content for old, but have begun to wonder what you are missing by not learning more about the application.

- You are an outside consultant brought in to work with people in the marketing department who have absolutely no idea how to refine a concept, crystallize an idea, or shape words into a message.

- You are hired to help terrified public speakers learn not to throw up all over themselves when in front of an audience.

- You work with the executives of your firm, and no matter how great the work is that you give to them before they board the plane, by the time they touch down at their destination, they've mauled your slide deck.

- You have worked your way into a position, created just for you, in which your expertise as a presentation professional is truly appreciated. You are given creative freedom and latitude, and are encouraged to cultivate your skills.

That last example is not fantasy; it only sounds too good to be true. There are just enough forward-thinking organizations and skilled presentation professionals to create optimism for the community at large.

In order for that community to grow and thrive, we need a universe of PowerPoint users who have moved past, as we describe in the first chapter, their 15 minutes worth of training.

That is the thrust of this work. You don't need help with the basics of PowerPoint. You know your way around the program. You need someone to speak frankly to you about the issues, the challenges, the joys, and indeed the perils associated with modern-day presentation creation and delivery. With this book, I accept that challenge.

How to Use This Book

There's an insulting headline for you. (*To use this book, start at the top of the page, read from left to right, and turn pages with your right hand...*) Proud authors like to insist that good books aren't used; they're read. But we in fields of technology know better. We know how people use computer books—lots of dog-eared pages, notes in the margin, index pages brutalized—and I'm fine with that.

My hope, however, is that you do find it to be a good read. By design, it is written very unevenly. Some chapters are just a few pages long, some over 30. Some topics we hammer and others we ignore. And I do not pretend that these 21 chapters are some sort of sterile, objective listing of "advanced tips," whatever that even means. This book is one person's view of the functions and nuances of PowerPoint that seem particularly relevant. It is full of bias and subjectivity and you are invited to disagree with it. In fact, if you agree with everything that I say here, its value is probably diminished.

In choosing my three editors, it was practically a prerequisite that they disagree with me on occasion, and when they did, I insisted that they write up their thoughts for me to include as a sidebar. As a result, these pages alternate between first-person singular and plural enough to drive a grammarian nuts, but that is my prerogative. There are times when I speak for the team...there are times when I speak on behalf of a community of thousands. And there are times when I feel as if I'm on Survivor's Exile Island. It's all good.

But no book should be an island—it's challenging enough to ask static pages to cover a medium of motion. And that is why we consider the book's web site, www.betterppt.com, to be a full partner in this endeavor. You'll see our constant references in the margins to files that you can download, view, and dissect, and most of the time, the filename mirrors the name of the particular figure or illustration.

There are no appendices to know about and there is no particular order in which you need to read this. **Part One** is where we bring the big hurt. We share our research and our conclusions about all that is wrong with the presentations industry and the software that is at its helm. Hopefully before the onset of depression, **Part Two** offers solutions to all of the pain we uncover in the chapters that precede it. **Part Three** is devoted to skills and strategies that anyone can adopt to help become a better public speaker, whether you are a natural at it or not. And **Part Four** steps up the volume considerably and covers several truly advanced topics and ideas for you to indulge in.

What Version Do You Need?

In many cases, it matters little what version of PowerPoint you use, and we encounter hundreds of presentation designers every year still using version 2000. A good designer needs only a blank slide; a good presenter could use a 1993 copy of Harvard Graphics.

Having said that, we'll make version 2000 users drool over some of the advanced techniques possible with a more current version, which we define to be version XP or later. Unless we say otherwise, all of the steps outlined and screen images shown are of version 2003.

The more interesting question is how to handle version 2007, released to the public when I was somewhere in the middle of Chapter 10. The still-brand-new release shows tremendous evolution in many critical areas, especially in graphics handling and slide mastering. However, corporate wheels being what they are and user preferences favoring the familiar over the new, we know that a small fraction of our readers will move to it any time soon. Therefore, we generally contain discussions and coverage of version 2007 to dedicated sections and extended sidebars.

We'd like to hear from you when you move to the current release.

If I have written this book correctly, it will prove to be bad for my business as a presentations consultant. A good chunk of my time as a hired gun is spent retraining, or untraining, to be precise. Many of the people with whom I work have read the reference guide and have taken some sort of introductory course, but never really learned any rules or guidelines for using the software.

By the time they bring me in, their slides often have dozens of unused placeholders, text boxes with bullets stuffed into them, random applications of animation, and multiple backgrounds.

Before I can teach them anything new, I have to strip off all of the old. I intend to provide you with the strategies, the techniques and the tools for becoming completely proficient with the projects that you need to produce. I intend to leave you with a more complete understanding of how the program operates. And I intend for you to not have to rely upon consultants like me as often.

I guess you could say that this book attempts to reduce by half my billable hours.

♦

Finally, the wonders of print on demand are numerous, chief among them the agility with which we can print new versions...perhaps starring you. If you: a) have created a presentation that illustrates a technique discussed herein; b) disagree with an assertion that we make; c) have an alternative technique to propose; d) want to suggest a topic for us to cover or expand upon; or e) just want to comment on a passage, please write to me at betterppt@altman.com or at the betterppt.com web site. We will not hesitate to include noteworthy commentary in an upcoming version, which, if sales go well, could be as early as next month...

Part One

The Pain

It was not the original vision to author a work of pessimism and it remains my hope that you will not view this book that way. Despite the somewhat bawdy title, which excites to no end those who wear marketing hats, I maintain that the ultimate message contained in these 267 pages is enabling and optimistic.

Nonetheless, first there are dues to pay. As good friend and messaging guru Jim Endicott likes to remind us, good storytelling is often about first identifying the pain. And as tennis great Martina Navratilova once said to me personally, "No pain...no gain." She was talking about physical fitness, not creating slides, but I couldn't pass up a chance to name drop...

Chapter 1

The 15-Minute Syndrome

If only I could earn the proverbial nickel for every time I have heard the following. It could be any setting in which the conversation might turn to PowerPoint, which in my case, is a frequent occurrence.

"Oh," the person says, in response to almost any remark made about the software. "PowerPoint is easy. I learned it in 15 minutes."

Let's start by acknowledging that the statement is generally true: PowerPoint is not difficult to pick up and begin using. Both of my daughters created slides for school projects before the age of 10, and indeed, a reasonably astute grownup can begin making slides within 15 minutes.

Microsoft might have you believe that this is a virtue of the software. In fact, it is bad. It is very, very bad.

Who Are These People??

Creating a presentation can be an extraordinarily creative experience, but it rarely starts out that way. And that is because most PowerPoint users do not start out in a creative field. They start out elsewhere in the Office suite. They are Excel crunchers, Outlook gurus, Access junkies. They are used to software with a steeper learning curve and a point of entry that requires much more effort before they can do much of anything. When they encounter PowerPoint and discover that they can begin using the program with effect in 15 minutes, they are like kids with new toys.

But again, this is not a good thing; it's a bad thing. These people declare themselves proficient after their requisite 15 minutes. These same people who get really good at their 15-minute skill set call themselves advanced. And those who get really fast at these same skills call themselves gurus.

But they don't get beyond those first 15 minutes of skills. And then they go forth and commit high crimes against innocent business-people everywhere. Yup...Death by PowerPoint.

We point our finger of accusation at both of the two main camps that we speak to in this book: those who create presentation content and those who deliver presentations. Often, one person wears both hats, but there is plenty of blame to go around: inexperienced content creators and ill-equipped presenters both contribute to the poor reputation endured by the software and the presentation industry in general.

Missing from the equation, of course, is the creative component. And you can't fault the typical number-crunching, word-processing Office user for not grasping that. These software programs are tools, wielded to perform tasks. You learn the tool well enough to perform the task, you go home for the day, and what happens in the cubicle stays in the cubicle.

But PowerPoint is different. With PowerPoint, you practice your craft in public, and this craft is forever linked with death and taxes as the three things humans fear most.

This is much more than the converted Excel user bargained for. It's possible, make that likely, that she had no experience at all speaking before a group; she simply taught herself how to make bullet slides.

And herein lies the biggest disconnect of all. The company that this innocent Excel-cum-PowerPoint user works for might spend millions of dollars on its brand. Expensive design firms to create glossy brochures...P.R. firms with more names on their door than law firms, hired to spin messages...high-powered marketing firms to ensure maximum exposure.

And this same company then sends someone out with 15 minutes of proficiency to make what will likely be a company's first impression: the presentation in a boardroom.

Why Is This Happening?

In the 1990s, Canada's Corel Corporation was flying high in the graphics world, owning the most heralded and most popular graphics program around, CorelDraw. Back in 1993, Version 4.0 added two programs to the suite: Chart and Show, to facilitate the creation of graphs and the animation of same.

They went nowhere, they were full of bugs, and most Draw users ignored them. Two years later, they were out of the suite altogether,

Figure 1.1
Corel's charting program was ahead of its time and not ready for prime time, but the graphic artists and illustrators who dabbled with it back in 1993 produced some very nice work.

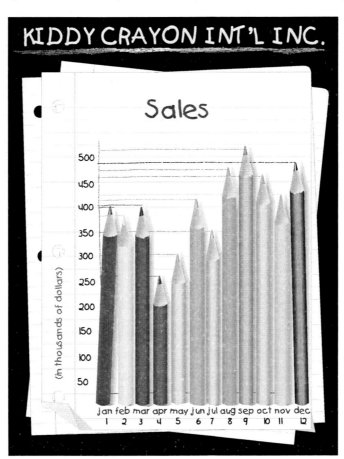

banished to small footnotes in the history of a smallish software maker. But a few users did dabble with them and their creations were quite impressive, as you can see in Figure 1.1. They were like nothing that any PowerPoint slide or Harvard Graphics chart (remember that?) ever produced.

This was perhaps the first time that a presentation tool was placed into the hands of a creative professional, and this little story from the past speaks volumes about the dilemma that the presentation community faces today. The issue is two-pronged:

- People are thrust into a position of being the company's creative force even though they do not have a background in the arts or in a creative field.

- Those who do have a creative background and are capable of producing excellent work with PowerPoint don't have a place in their company's org chart.

I would also like a nickel for every time that I have met a PowerPoint user with an obscure and obtuse title, or simply the "admin." Not to impugn in any way the workforce of administrative professionals; the title does not and should not imply that a graphically talented person is holding it.

Companies have simply not made enough of an effort to identify, define, and cultivate the role of the presentation professional. Therefore, it usually is assigned in haphazard fashion to anyone willing to step up to the plate, including the person who is simply good with Microsoft Office.

◆

Have I described you yet? Odds are, I'm in trouble one way or the other. If I have identified you as the person thrust into the role of PowerPoint jockey, I've either offended you or made you defensive. If you are the creative professional honing your craft with presentations, I've reminded you of your biggest frustration and now you're mad at me. There's pain in this part of the book for me, too!

There's hope for all of us...but we're not yet done with the pain. In other words, if I didn't offend you this chapter, I have several more opportunities upcoming.

Chapter 2

The Cram-Everything-In Obsession

Did you watch *Super Size Me*, the documentary on over-eating at McDonalds? ("A film of epic portions," www.supersizeme.com). Both of my daughters vowed that they would never eat another Big Mac again, and one of them has actually kept that vow to this day, some 16 months later. It espouses one of America's most robust sentiments: bigger is better, and more is more better.

I just got through watching an episode of The Apprentice, where a handsome, well-dressed twenty-something pleaded his case to Donald Trump by reciting every business slogan he could possibly think of, as fast as he possibly could, interspersed with the robotic "I'll be great for your organization, Mr. Trump" at every breath. And it worked: Trump fired the other guy.

This is a very real phenomenon in today's culture—the sense that it's better to say everything than risk forgetting to say the one thing that you really need to say. And nowhere is this more evident than in the typical slides that project onto the whiteboards and white screens of America today.

This plays out in a fairly predictable way by those who prepare their own slides for a presentation:

- They sit down at their desk.

- They open PowerPoint.

- They start thinking of every point that they need to make.

- Soon they start thinking of how they are going to make each point.

End result: they have written a speech.

I want to be fair here: If you have little or no experience speaking before a group of people, you have no idea that this is the wrong approach to take. This might seem like a perfectly logical way to pre-pare: write down what you want to say and then say it. And hey, there's this software program that will show you everything that you've written down, so your audience can see it, too.

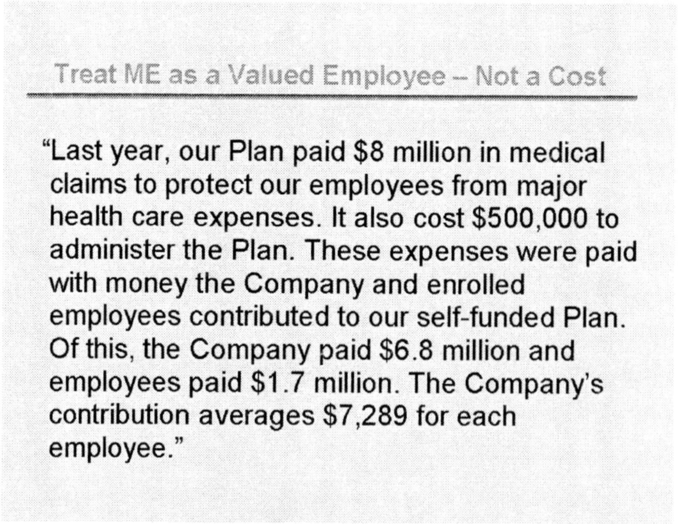

Figure 2.1

This slide says everything the speaker wants to say, so what's the problem?

> Treat ME as a Valued Employee – Not a Cost
>
> "Last year, our Plan paid $8 million in medical claims to protect our employees from major health care expenses. It also cost $500,000 to administer the Plan. These expenses were paid with money the Company and enrolled employees contributed to our self-funded Plan. Of this, the Company paid $6.8 million and employees paid $1.7 million. The Company's contribution averages $7,289 for each employee."

This is not such a bad proposition for the uninitiated public speaker; as we all know, it's a horrible proposition for her audience. The woman from Scottsdale Arizona probably thought she was on the right track when she perpetrated the slide shown in Figure 2.1. It said everything she wanted to say.

Figure 2.2
What a difference five minutes can make. You might actually stop and read this slide now.

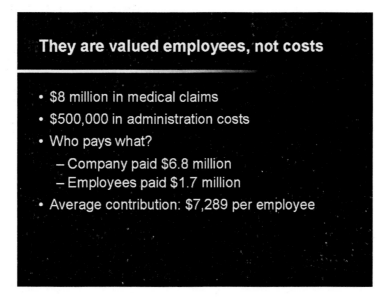

> ### They are valued employees, not costs
>
> - $8 million in medical claims
> - $500,000 in administration costs
> - Who pays what?
>   - Company paid $6.8 million
>   - Employees paid $1.7 million
> - Average contribution: $7,289 per employee

No question about it: one of today's most acute pain points is when speakers use their slides as notes. In many cases, it is because they have no idea that the Notes view exists.

This leads to the first of several universal axioms that we will put forth across these pages. Universal Axiom No. 1 goes like this:

> **If a slide contains complete sentences, it is practically impossible for even the most accomplished presenters to avoid reading the entire slide word for word.**

Watch for it the next time you attend a presentation: the more verbiage a slide contains, the more likely is the speaker to read all of it. Talk about your double-whammy. We discuss strategies to work around this in Chapter 13, and they are important, because Universal Axiom No. 1 leads directly into Universal Axiom No. 2:

> **When you read your slides word for word, you sound like an idiot.**

Figure 2.2 is the result of a five-minute makeover. We did nothing more than apply a solid black background, light gray text, a simple rule, and the parsing out of main ideas into bullets. If you take 10 seconds, you'll get the gist of what this presentation is about, but you probably would not have invested even one second trying to sift through the original slide.

More important, we might stand a chance of hearing the real person come out if she speaks to the second slide, as opposed to the drone who would have read the first slide. Gone is the compulsion to recite the slide verbatim; now she'll have to collect her thoughts and deliver them. Scary? Perhaps at first. But the five-minute slide makeover will also make her over into a better presenter.

But we're getting ahead of ourselves. First, more pain...

Chapter 3

Look at Me!!

It was the fall of 2003 and life as I knew it was about to change forever. We were in Tucson AZ for the debut of PowerPoint Live, and Glen Millar had traveled from Australia to lead a session on animation. Glen is a brilliant designer of presentations who has dreamed up and forgotten more techniques than you or I will learn in our lifetimes.

And he was upfront about what he was about to show his audience. "You're about to see some really gratuitous stuff here," he said in his Down Under drawl, to which the audience laughed. "In order to discover the potential of what the software can do, sometimes you just have to experiment."

With similar irreverence, the slide was entitled "Absolute Nonsense," and it looked like Figure 3.1. You'll want to take a trip to the betterppt.com web site and download 03-01.ppt to see what Glen showed his audience that day. Gears turning, pistons pumping, paddles flapping, balls bouncing...all controlled by PowerPoint animation.

To download any of the files referenced in this book, point your browser to www.betterppt.com/[name of file].ppt. You'll be prompted to choose between opening the file in your browser window or downloading it, and in the case of heavily animated files, it's best to download the file to your computer and open it in PowerPoint.

Each of the elements on this slide are carefully timed to become part of a working, almost organic, system of motion. Most in the audience had never seen anything like this and had never considered the use of animation in this way. If you look up *epiphany* in the dictionary, it really should reference Glen Millar's October 18, 2003 workshop on animation.

Figure 3.1
When the audience saw Glen's animation contraption in 2003, their lives changed. They saw an entirely new dimension to the potential of attracting the attention of their audience.

The buzz lasted all day; I knew the affects of this presentation would be more lasting. And I was a bundle of conflict. After all, what better advertisement for a conference in its rookie season than 200 disciples returning to their colleagues and saying, "I can't wait to show you what I learned at PowerPoint Live!"

But the specter loomed of these same disciples returning to their places of work and wasting not a moment finding an occasion to use their new skills. This tendency is remarkably human and cuts across all disciplines and all ages. My wife Becky and I can remember as if it happened yesterday the moment that our six-month-old daughter Erica discovered that she could flex a muscle in her throat and emit a sound. The cause and effect relationship was captivating to her and nothing short of a tranquilizer would stop her from demonstrating her new skill that night. And I'll show you the very essay in which our other daughter Jamie, then in third grade, discovered adjectives.

In software parlance, I refer to this as use of a feature based on recency of discovery, not appropriateness to the task. You use it because you just learned it. Rounded corners on rectangles back in the desktop publishing boom of 1986…dressing up your C:\> prompt in 1988…drop shadows in 1993…related database fields in 1997…Excel pivot tables in 2000…and "absolute nonsense" in 2003. The urge to place into operation that which you have just learned might be one of the finest human traits ever. However, when you practice your craft in public, it has potentially lasting implications. You can usually tell when a person has just learned, say, how to make bullets go dim after appearing, or how to make a title fly in letter by letter. When you see the effect in action, but it has no context or purpose whatsoever, there's a good chance that recency of discovery is the driving force behind its use.

I should note that we who considered ourselves Glen's colleagues that day were not left out of the epiphany. When he showed a little-known trick of hiding the background and showing pieces of it through other objects (see Figure 3.2), he sent us all scurrying to our notepads or notebooks.

To this day, many of us on that debut teaching team in 2003 still look for excuses to use this background trick, even if it is not suitable to the context of the presentation. We too cannot resist saying "look at me!" in public.

By its nature, PowerPoint is an extroverted activity. People turn to it for the purpose of communication—often in person, often to large audiences. You put your ego on the line when you do this, so it helps to have a healthy one. In fact, showing off is almost part of the essential nature of the discipline and should not be viewed as an entirely negative trait.

But there are right ways and wrong ways to get attention, and there must always be purpose behind it. This chapter's pain is brought to

Figure 3.2
Even the experts at PowerPoint Live learned something new when Glen Millar showed how to place a photo on the background, cover it up with a full-sized rectangle, create an object on top of the rectangle (the ellipse), and fill it with the background image.

you by the compulsion to add gimmicks to PowerPoint presentations when there is absolutely no reason to do so. *The fact that you just learned how to do it does not change anything.* If it doesn't contribute to the message, it has no place on your slides.

Chapter 11 discusses some of the healthier ways to show off in public.

Chapter 4

Bitter Backgrounds

There is a continuum on the pain pendulum that I would characterize as follows:

Not so bad .... Bland content
Mildly bad......... Bland speaker
Really bad......... Annoying content
Flaming bad ...... Annoying speaker
The worst .... Annoying everything

We're not sure where bad backgrounds fit, but this much is certain: little is more frustrating than slides that could have legitimate appeal but cannot be easily read. If you know that a presentation sucks, you can leave the room or start texting your friends ("omg this sux ur lucky ur not here...l8r"). When the speaker is good and the content actually interesting, it is doubly frustrating when the visuals work against you.

Invariably, this happens when content creators louse up with their backgrounds, and this usually can be traced to a fundamental lack of understanding about what makes a good background.

Backgrounds Shouldn't Be in the Foreground

We can put this entire problem to rest with one sentence:

Put white type on a black background.

Done. Problem solved. Stop reading, go home. If you're already home, go out to a movie. In the history of presentations, no deal has ever been lost, no contract not awarded, no grant not granted because a presenter used white text on a black background. It's the ultimate chicken soup for PowerPoint: It couldn't hurt. (That's pronounced "it cuddnt hoit," for those looking to brush up on their Jewish dialect.)

At the same time, we pundits have been telling you that photos can make a world of difference for your presentations, so it's no surprise that many of you choose to integrate them into the backgrounds of your slides. The problem is that sometimes you choose photos that are too good!

Witness Figure 4.1, downloaded from the AbleStock photo library. This is a nice contemporary business image, taken from a cool angle. It would vibrate well with any businessperson today.

I would love to use it in a presentation...

I could envision burning type into it for dramatic effect...

I might pan across it...

I'd have a blast setting it to music...

Figure 4.1
Great photo, lousy background

But I wouldn't use it as my presentation's background, certainly not in its present form. It steals the show; it refuses to stay in the background. It does the one thing that you don't want your background to do: it takes attention away from your foreground—your text. Once you do that, you're done.

Now if the photo *is* the message, that's different. If the photo conveys your message without the need for text, that's the holy grail of presenting! But that doesn't happen very often, and most of us need to be content with integrating a photo with our text-based message.

Figure 4.2
This photo has too much contrast and too many points of interest. Bullets don't stand a chance and you cannot pick any one color of text that would have sufficient contrast against this photo.

Looking for Contrast in All the Wrong Places

Integrating standard bullets into this photo would be exceedingly difficult. Where would you put them? Figure 4.2 shows the folly of trying to approach this design from a conventional perspective—there's no traditional layout that is going to give you readability.

The culprit here is contrast and it is the single most misunderstood concept among those just starting to get experience blending imagery with standard PowerPoint content. If you had to sit through 30 slides that looked like this, you wouldn't care if it were the incarnate of Albert Einstein as the speaker. You'd tune out.

The most important interplay between foreground and background is contrast. In short, you want a lot of it! You want dark text against a light background or vice-versa. People who had this mantra hammered into their heads sometimes go on auto-pilot and hear the singular message "look for high contrast." They find photos with high contrast and then get frustrated when their designs don't work properly.

A photo that has high contrast is going to fly in the face of your efforts to create appropriate contrast between foreground and background, and Figure 4.2 illustrates this problem perfectly. In order for you to rely on your background photo to provide good contrast with your foreground content, that photo must have low contrast, not high contrast.

As someone who acts as a commentator to the presentation community, I love that content creators are beginning to integrate visuals into their work. As with any other discipline, there are right ways and wrong ways to do this.

See Chapter 10 for an in-depth exploration of integrating photos, mastering contrast, and understanding transparency.

Chapter 5

The Scourge that is Custom Animation

There I sat, not three feet away, and I couldn't believe what I was hearing. I the consultant, he the client, trying to determine the best course of action to take with a slide whose content was not communicating the right message.

"It seems to me as if we're not quite getting to the central point," I said to him. "It's not just that you save your customers time, they also benefit from a sales team that speaks a dozen different languages. I think we need to make that point stronger."

I swear I'm not making this up, his response to me. "How about if we make those bullets fly in when I say it?"

"_____"

"Rick? Are you okay?"

Okay, so that last part of the exchange was made up. I didn't actually go comatose. No doubt, though, a camera focused on me would have captured a look of utter bewilderment at the notion that gratuitous animation applied to a clump of words was actually the answer. However poorly this reflected on my client's sensibilities, it was even more insulting to his theoretical audience whom he hoped would be persuaded to take action as a result of bullets flying on screen.

That, in one 30-second exchange, sums up our national obsession. We prefer television to radio, movies to books, and slides that move to ones that are static. We learned this at our first conference when the seminar on animation overflowed into the hotel foyer; now we offer that session in the general ballroom that can hold over 200 and we don't bother offering any other seminars at the same time.

The irony of this situation is delicious. Earnest PowerPoint users are so completely taken with animation, they would gladly stand in the back of a hotel ballroom for 60 minutes in the hope of picking up a new trick or two. And at the same time, every single poll ever taken about PowerPoint's most annoying characteristics (Google "Power-Point" and "annoying" to see how many have been conducted) lists bad animation in the top five, without fail.

This much is clear: Whatever skills people learn in those first 15 minutes, restraint and good taste with animation are not among them.

Your Audience is at Your Mercy

There is a reason why this topic strikes such a raw nerve among those who suffer through poorly-crafted presentations, and to understand it, we will now introduce Universal Axiom No. 3:

> **When something moves on screen, your audience
> has no choice but to watch it.**

This is a response that occurs at a subconscious level; you cannot help yourself. On summer evenings, I like to read on our front porch, and anytime that a house on our street turns a light on, I must look up. I know exactly what occurs in my peripheral vision and I know that it is of no consequence to me…and yet I must look at it. I'm like a moth. If you paid attention to this, I predict you would notice the same behavior in yourself.

In response to a skeptic at a recent seminar, I prepared the following experiment. I stood off to the side of the room, about 30 feet from the screen, and began to talk about this. In mid-sentence, careful not

Figure 5.1
For better or for worse, you have no choice but to watch objects as they move on screen.

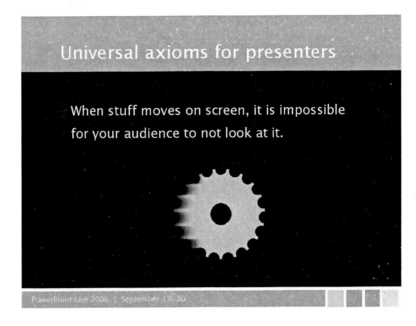

to take my eyes off of the audience, I sent a gear flying across the screen, just as you see in Figure 5.1.

Everyone looked.

"Hey, I'm over here," I said playfully, as the audience returned their gaze to me. Five seconds later, a smiley face appeared on screen and then drifted off.

Everyone looked.

"You see what I mean? You can't help it!"

At that point, I had an ellipse appear and disappear in a blink. There wasn't enough time for anyone to take their eyes off of me, but they all still saw the flashing ellipse in their peripheral vision. Everyone laughed and I knew that I had made my point.

Your Covenant with the Audience

This implies a tremendous obligation on our part as presenters and content creators. Our industry needs its own variation of the Hippocratic Oath: Above all, we shall practice no excess.

If we know that our audience is compelled to track movement on the slide, it is incumbent on us to make sure that we use that power wisely and responsibly.

That rarely happens.

More likely, inexperienced PowerPoint users apply animation in knee-jerk fashion. If they haven't applied animation to something on the slide, they feel as if they haven't done their jobs. Our creative editor, Sandra Johnson, was told this quite succinctly by the CEO of a major corporation: "the slide is incomplete without animation."

I don't have to go further than the adjacent bedroom, the one occupied by my 14-year-old daughter, to witness the dynamic first-hand. We live in an environment in which multimedia distractions are part of the background noise. I truly believe that today's teenagers feel somehow disfunctional without them. It seems that we have created that same environment for our presentations. If a slide consists solely of bullets, we are compelled to animate them. An otherwise ordinary ruling line below a title is inflated in importance by a Fly In From Left. Slide transitions can't just wipe; they must dissolve. We have

How Much is Too Much?

Some animations are worse than others, and now you know the barometer by which it should be measured: are audience members forced to track motion across the slide? The ones that move the most are the most potentially intrusive.

We have prepared the Official Rick Altman Pain Scale for you, to be consulted whenever you feel the urge to make something move:

Animation	From / To	Pain Quotient (5 is the worst)
Boomerang, Spiral, Swivel	Anywhere	6
Fly	From side to side	5
Fly	From bottom to top	4
Zoom Out	Anywhere	4
Fly	From left edge one inch onto the slide	3
Zoom In	Anywhere	3
Wipe Slowly	n/a	2
Wipe Quickly	n/a	0
Fade	n/a	0

created the implication that if an object just sits there, it must not be very important. It must move; it must exude some level of energy.

And every single time we do it, our audience is compelled to watch.

◆

Chapter 11 continues the discussion of proper use of animation. When done correctly, animation can be a beautiful thing.

Exercising restraint with animation is not easy, as thousands of annoyed members of daily PowerPoint audiences will readily attest. And of all of the characteristics that define pain, misused animation is one of the most important to avoid. When you use animation gratuitously, you call into question your own sensibility. This threatens your entire reason for being up there in front of them.

Because we are environmentally conscious, we have chosen not to kill a tree writing about all of the annoying animations that exist within PowerPoint, but you get the idea.

Animations that force your audience to track an object all the way across, up, or down the slide are the most invasive. The more lateral or vertical movement, the more visual tracking is required of them.

If an object flies all the way from the right to the standard starting point for bullets on the left side, that's really bad. An object that flies in from the left to that same point is not as bad. Zooming Out could fill the entire screen—that's bad—but zooming in does not grow the object beyond the size that it is ultimately going to be, and that's not so bad.

Similarly, Wipe and Fade take care of their business inside the boundaries of the object. They do not require that the audience track any motion across the slide, and as such, they earn a place at the bottom of the Pain Scale, where no pain exists. We said this earlier, we're saying it again, and we'll surely say it several more times: you can't be hurt by Wipe or Fade.

◆

Meanwhile, you had better have a very good reason to use Spiral, Boomerang, or Pinwheel. And if you ever find a legitimate reason to apply it to text, please email me at you're_lying@bull****.com.

Chapter 6

Can PowerPoint Make You Stupid?

One of the most inflammatory ideas circulating among PowerPoint skeptics has received quite a bit of credible press in the past few years. In a widely-circulated 2004 article, New York Times columnist Clive Thompson all but blamed the Shuttle Columbia accident on the use of PowerPoint. (www.betterppt.com/shuttle).

And the ever-bombastic Edward Tufte has essentially made a living out of attributing many of society's communication problems to Microsoft's venerable slide-making tool.

It's hard to imagine that a software program could be credited with something as profound as affecting one's intellect, but read on—there is a real dynamic at work here, making up the final chapter identifying PowerPoint pain.

Where Good Ideas Go to Die

Two years ago, a client named Lon came to me for assistance with a keynote address he was giving to a group of professional tennis teachers. These teachers were working with some of the most talented junior players in Northern California, so they were well beyond teaching the fundamentals of tennis. Their jobs were to turn these kids into seasoned athletes, help them land college scholarships, and maybe prepare them for the pro tour.

Lon had some innovative ideas to share with these teachers about how to turn kids with raw talent into strong competitors and winners. Over a beer, he was amazing, fluent with such heady concepts as the ideal performance state, living in the present moment, and his most novel theory, having to do with calming the mind to maximize the body's energy.

I'm a tennis player, and even though I barely understood what he was saying, I loved hearing him speak about it. These were novel and bold ideas about helping exceptionally talented athletes reach beyond their potential. When his ideas were flowing, he was a joy to listen to.

Now he needed to corral all of his wonderful ideas into a 60-minute after-dinner talk, and he wanted to show me the PowerPoint slides that he had created so far. My first reaction surprised him.

"Why do you need to show slides?"

"I'm sure that they're expecting it."

Figure 6.1

Can this slide help a coach talk to other coaches? Not likely...

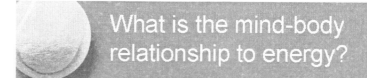

What is the mind-body relationship to energy?

- A way of helping athletes understand their own rhythms
- Achieving focus through better balance of life forces
- Getting to the Now quicker

Figure 6.2
This slide did not inhibit Lon's ability to articulate his thoughts.

"I'm expecting you to do the unexpected."

Once he untangled himself from my circular argument, he insisted that slides would make his talk go smoother.

He was wrong. Figure 6.1 showed his weak attempt to fit his thoughts onto a bullet slide. It sounded like mumbo-jumbo, something his ideas never did when he spoke about them informally. Worse, when he practiced his speech with his slides, he found himself trying to explain the meaning of the words on the slides, instead of the thoughts in his head.

Ultimately, I convinced Lon to go with Figure 6.2 instead. His ideas were more than enough to carry the hour; all he needed were a good image to evoke an emotional response and a few main topics to lead the way.

This was the classic example of good ideas getting torpedoed by PowerPoint. Lon's ideas were far too complex to be contained within one title and three bullet points. Most good ideas can't survive such a boiling down, yet that is the default medium for sharing ideas in public. When smart people try to represent their good ideas with such a limiting medium, they come off sounding less smart.

PowerPoint does indeed dumb them down.

Talking Points Can Create Talking Heads

Unless presenters practice with their material and with the medium, even simple and succinct bullets can derail them. I witnessed a good example of this just the other day, watching a volleyball match on ESPN. (Two sports anecdotes in one chapter? Get used to it! Ask anyone who knows me: sports is my metaphor for everything in life.)

Calling the action were Chris Marlowe, an experienced play-by-play professional, and Vince, a former Olympic player. Each of them was required, at various times during the broadcast, to comment on a statistic or a notable fact being displayed in a graphic.

One of Vince's assignments was to discuss the factors that he thought were significant during a particular match. The graphic displayed three items: return of serve, ability to set a double-block, and free-ball passing. With only a few months of experience as a television commentator and no formal training or background, Vince did nothing more than read, word for word, the three items in the graphic. He would have done far better if he were instructed to describe, in his own words, the three key elements of the match. The audience didn't need to see the graphic, but when ESPN showed it, it paralyzed Vince, reducing him to a cue-card reader.

Chris Marlowe is much more experienced in these matters. The graphic he was asked to elaborate on showed how many times UCLA, the top-ranked team in the nation, had won games after being down game point. While the graphic showed the percentages and statistics, Marlowe said, "You don't win four championships in six years without playing the big points well, and here is why so many consider UCLA to be one of history's most successful teams."

Now that's the way to speak to bullet points! Marlowe didn't insult his audience's literacy by reading the graphic. Instead, he made the moment greater than the sum of its parts by telling us something more than just the raw facts.

Even though he is on live television and the stakes are high, Marlowe has an advantage over the person giving a speech. As a play-by-play announcer, Marlowe does not know what is about to happen, he does not work off of a script, and often he doesn't have any idea what he is going to say next. That promotes spontaneity and creativity, two of the most important ingredients of good public speaking.

While inexperienced with talking points, Vince proved to be an acute analyst of the game. When allowed to simply react to what he was watching, he was articulate, relaxed, and confident.

I suspect there are many executives and corporate speechmakers who are like Lon or Vince: astute, well-spoken, but ultimately hampered by the unspoken requirement that all high-tech speeches be accompanied by a PowerPoint slide show. I had lunch recently with a Silicon Valley-based executive and he summed the situation up perfectly. First, he acknowledged that most of his colleagues are too busy to spend more than a half-hour working on their slides.

"Is it so important that they have slides?" I asked.

"Today," he replied, "you can't give a talk in this business without showing slides."

"But what can you do in 30 minutes?"

"Copy and paste your notes into the bullet holders."

"But if you just turn your notes into slides, your slides will be the same as what you say."

"That's right."

"That's sad."

"That's right."

You can't give a talk today without showing slides. Those are some of the most distressing words I have heard all year. *Too busy to spend more than 30 minutes on their slides.* This is yet another example of knee-jerk software practice: Use determined by availability, not need. Executives with good speaking skills don't need slides as they talk, and if they do, their slides should elaborate on their ideas, not repeat them. And executives who lack speaking skills make the situation worse with bad slides that compel them to read their speech instead of deliver it.

Here is another excellent-to-awful continuum for you, to go with the one in Chapter 4:

Best Presentation: Truly excellent speaker, great ideas, and slides that amplify on the points made, instead of repeating them.

Very Good: Truly excellent speaker, great ideas, and no slides.

Still Okay: Excellent speaker, redundant slides that don't add anything.

Not so Good: Bad speaker, good slides

Pretty Bad: Bad speaker, no slides

Dreadful: Bad speaker, redundant slides

PowerPoint is capable of turning good presenters into bad presenters and bad presenters into dreadful ones.

The Wrong Place to Start

Where do people go wrong? Often, their fatal errors are made in the first 10 seconds of a project: they put the mouse in their hand way too early in the process.

Even though it doesn't involve PowerPoint, a recent experience I had crystallized this issue for me. On a flight home a few years ago, I sat next to two businessmen, both using their notebook computers. I couldn't resist spying on them.

One of them was using CorelDraw, a graphic drawing program that I have been using since its inception in the late 1980s. The other was composing in Microsoft Word. The man using Draw was producing some sort of flier or publicity sheet, and he was struggling. He kept creating objects and text strings, fiddling with them, and then deleting them. He appeared to have no direction or objective.

I couldn't see what the other man was writing about, but what struck me was that he spent half his time making notes on a yellow legal pad. Funny, I thought, why doesn't he just use Word to keep his notes, and I asked him that very thing.

> **"This is the way I've always done it,"** he said, **"and I can't break the habit. I always make my outlines longhand before writing."**

Well, the irony of this situation was delicious. The man who least needed to use pencil and paper before embarking on a computer-based project couldn't work without them, and the man who desperately needed to do a bit of sketching or scribbling was trying to create a drawing using an eraser head to move the cursor.

Why do we computer users do this to ourselves? I think I know the answer, but first, let's point out the obvious: When you embark on a task—any task—first you decide what it is you want to do, then you determine how you are going to do it, and then you do it. That's how people do things in real life. All too often, however, users of creative software, like CorelDraw or PowerPoint, go about everything bass-ackwards. They sit in front of the computer, place their hand on the mouse, and start creating objects, hoping that a finished piece will spontaneously occur. In no other aspect of their lives do they expect to achieve success in this manner, but they hold exempt from natural laws their relationship with their software applications.

People come to graphics and presentation software from so many different professions and pursuits, it's impossible to generalize about work habits. But there is one thing that is clear: Most users do not arrive at the software with a formal background in any creative field. They have not had significant experience with sketch pads, light tables, dark rooms, or any other traditional creative tool. Their software is likely the only tool for working on a creative project that they have been exposed to, so it's only natural that they would use it for the entirety of a project.

This was certainly the case with the man in 16C. He knew that he had to produce a flier on a particular topic, but I doubt that he started with much more direction than that. He kept drawing shapes, creating text, moving them around, stopping, thinking, stretching, rotating, filling, deleting, redrawing...and all the while growing visibly frustrated. He expected CorelDraw to act as his sketch pad, or better yet, to magically produce the flier for him.

We see this same dynamic among PowerPoint users, usually to the same detriment. The cold hard fact is that programs like CorelDraw, Photoshop, Dreamweaver, and PowerPoint are the wrong tools for the beginning phases of a project, totally wrong. This is not a criticism of PowerPoint and the others—let's please just acknowledge that these programs are finishing tools, not starting tools.

PowerPoint lets you do a lot of things quickly and easily, but sketching or roughing out a creative concept is not one of them. There's way too much temptation to make everything perfect, and that's exactly what you don't want to do at this stage. When starting work on a presentation, experienced content creators look to get ideas out as quickly as they think of them. This is the time to open the creative canal as wide as possible; it is not the time to be thinking of transitions, animation choices, backgrounds, or color schemes. In fact, it's not the time to be handling the mouse at all.

The man in 16A had the right idea. While only creating a word-processed document, he realized that he's better off mapping out his route on paper first. Even Word offers too many temptations to make a first draft perfect, what with spell and grammar checkers, document controls, and paragraph formatting tools. He just wanted a brain

Figure 6.3
Even the pros begin
with pencil and
paper, not with
slides.

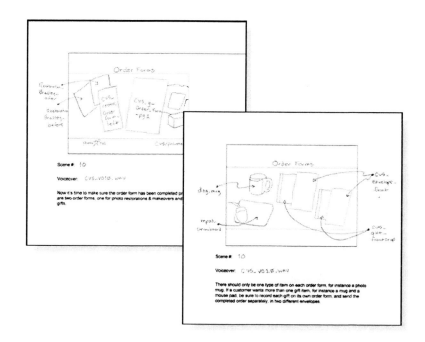

Figure 6.4
Proof positive that
your pre-slide
sketches don't have
to look
like much.

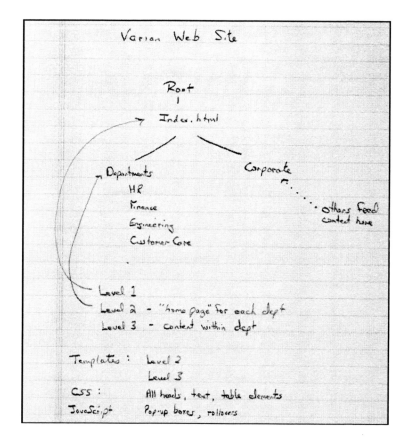

dump, and the best dumping ground is the legal pad. He didn't have very good handwriting; I doubt that he got an A in third grade penmanship. But that is of no consequence during the idea stage.

Figure 6.3 shows a sketch of a presentation prepared by Julie Terberg, one of the most prominent and talented presentation designers in the world. She is a regular at PowerPoint Live, where she shares her vast knowledge of design theory and how it is best applied to the presentation medium. Many in the audience were surprised when she showed this sketch, but in her own words, "I always start with pencil and paper. I'm freer that way."

Her sketches are probably nicer-looking than many of your or my finished products, but that is unimportant. Witness my chicken-scratching in Figure 6.4 about creating a PowerPoint-based tutorial on web-site design. It's a mess! But it is every bit as useful to me as Julie's sketches are to her.

It is not the product of your sketching that is so important to the process, it is the *act* of sketching. Sketching...doodling...free-associating...these are the secret ingredients to brilliance!

Kind of funny when you think of it. One of the secrets to using PowerPoint effectively is knowing when not to use it.

◆

As we conclude our definition of everything wrong with modern-day PowerPoint usage, we have already produced for you one recipe for creating pleasing and potentially effective presentations:

- Organize your thoughts away from your computer

- Use white text

- Create black backgrounds

- Use only wipes or fades

If you confine yourself to those four practices, if you don't read past this point, if you *throw this book in the trash right now*, I'll be satisfied that we have reduced by one the number of people in the world who might produce annoying and obnoxious presentations.

Part Two

The Solution

If you're still with me after the first six chapters, you're in need of a good catharsis, and the rest of this book seeks to provide just that. If you have reached the conclusion that yes, most PowerPoint presentations do indeed suck, rest assured that there are solutions at hand.

We won't shy away from the direct tone that we adopted in Part 1; each of us remains just one poor choice away from creating a horrible presentation. But from here on, our objective is to arm you with the tools, strategies, and principles behind the creation of truly excellent presentations.

Chapter 7

Surviving Bullets

We have chosen the order of these first few chapters carefully. Exhaustive articles have been written on the evils of bullets. My friend Cliff Atkinson wrote an entire book, and a good one, *Beyond Bullet Points*, espousing alternative approaches to creating content slides.

I disagree with neither the sentiment nor the philosophy behind this argument. Presentation content creators who go on auto-pilot often end up in trouble. The world does not need any more bullet slides in order to prosper.

But we have to be pragmatic here. Irrespective of your opinion about bullets, there is no escape from them. They are as inevitable as colds in the winter and mosquitoes in the summer.

Even if you wanted to move beyond creating bullet slides, there are two reasons why you might not be able to:

1) Many of you, we predict almost half, create presentations for others, in many cases your bosses or clients, and you are not at liberty to make those kinds of wholesale design changes.

2) We mean no disrespect, but it's possible that you lack the design expertise to achieve it.

Instead of trying to eliminate bullets from your slides, you might be better off trying to make your bullets as effective as possible, and that is the focus of this chapter.

Three Words

What if a law were passed prohibiting bullets from exceeding three words in length? Could you abide by it? Perhaps not, but humor me on this one, because it stands as one of the best exercises you can do, whether you are the presenter, the content creator, or both.

▼ This section pertains to presentations delivered live via a presenter. Presentations designed to be sent electronically and read on screen by the recipient are not subject to the same verbiage issues. In short, it's okay to be wordy with a self-running presentation, because those are the only words available to the recipient.

Fresh off all that pain in Part 1, you probably don't need a reminder about Universal Axioms 1 and 2, but you're getting one anyway:

If a slide contains complete sentences, it is practically impossible for even the most accomplished presenters to avoid reading them word for word.

And when you read your slides word for word, you sound like an idiot.

Figure 7.1 is a classic culprit. Somebody simply did an idea dump right into his or her slides, and anyone who tries to speak to this slide is doomed to sound like an idiot.

Before you read on, I want you to clean this slide up by mentally reducing each bullet point down to three words. I know, it's very hard to do! Ditch the vowels, jettison the pronouns, eliminate the flotsam.

Figure 7.1
Pity the poor presenter who has to work with this slide.

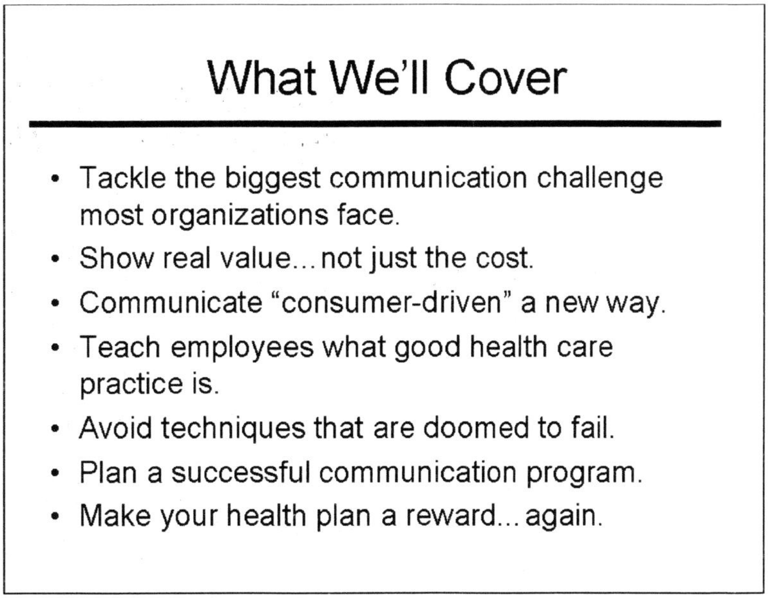

What We'll Cover

- Tackle the biggest communication challenge most organizations face.
- Show real value... not just the cost.
- Communicate "consumer-driven" a new way.
- Teach employees what good health care practice is.
- Avoid techniques that are doomed to fail.
- Plan a successful communication program.
- Make your health plan a reward... again.

Even with your sharpest knife, you might not be able to cut all the way down to three words, but the reward is in the effort. Several important things take place when you make an earnest attempt to get within three words:

Your slides are friendlier
With just that one task, you create slides that are much easier on the eyes of your audience. Visual fatigue is the silent killer of presentations. When you ask your audience to sit in a dimly-lit room for 30 or 60 minutes, their eyes are going to be the first to go. The more words each slide contains, the quicker the onset of fatigue. Fewer words, less fatigue. Your bullets might not be as descriptive, but that's okay—it's your job to do the describing.

Your pace improves
Something almost magical happens when you reduce the amount of words on a slide. Everything seems snappier. The slide draws more quickly, audience members absorb the information more efficiently, and you most likely project more energy.

You create intrigue
In three words, you are not going to be able to fully explain your points. But that's not bad; it's good. In fact, it's terrific! Without even trying to, you create mystique and intrigue. You invite audience members to use their imaginations. Once you get good at the three-word rule, you will become a better writer of bullets. You will begin

to write with color and humor; you could become coy, even flirta-tious. These literary techniques serve to command attention. They help to engage your audience on an emotional level. And that, my friends, is the holy grail of presenting.

You learn your material better

Of the many bad things associated with dumping complete sentences onto slides, perhaps the worst is how lazy it makes the presenter, whether it is you or someone for whom you create slides. Excess ver-biage sends a subtle but powerful message that you don't need to pre-pare as much, because everything you want to say is already there.

Parsing the words increases your burden as a presenter, but the effort is worth it. Adhering to the three-word rule forces you to learn your content at a level you otherwise might not have reached.

One of my favorite quotes about presenting comes from Mark Twain:

> **"If you want me to speak for an hour, I am ready today. If you want me to speak for just a few minutes, it will take me a few weeks to prepare."**

The three-word rule is a microcosm of this wonderful dynamic that Twain articulated. In order to get down to three words, you really need to study the text. You need to truly understand what you are trying to say and you need to pick three words that create the perfect backdrop for your ideas. Getting down to three words requires that you practically get intimate with your text.

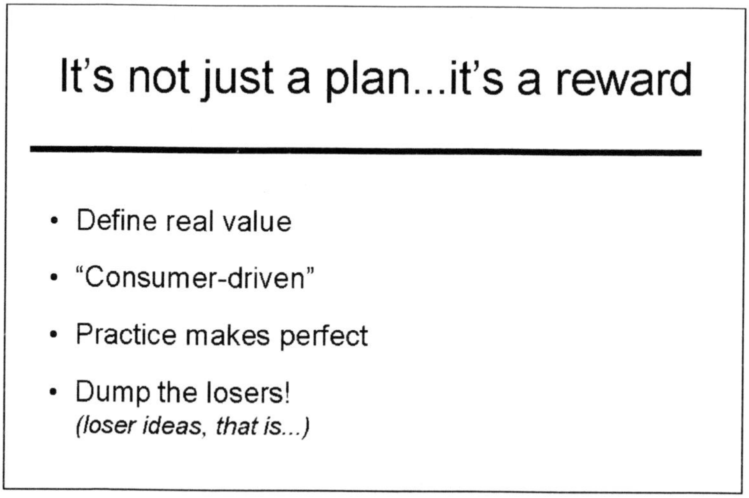

Figure 7.2
This slide no longer gets in the way. It frames the subjects and allows the presenter to find his or her natural speaking rhythm.

It's not just a plan...it's a reward

- Define real value
- "Consumer-driven"
- Practice makes perfect
- Dump the losers!
  (loser ideas, that is...)

Figure 7.2 shows our attempt at adhering to the three-word rule. You can see that we failed with one of the bullets, but the sum of our effort and our failures was an unqualified victory. The slide is much stronger now, and even though I don't know beans about the subject, having gone through this process, I feel as if I could almost present on it now.

A few things to note:

- We eliminated altogether the two bullets about communications. This is purely subjective, but good communication is so fundamental to this topic, it doesn't need a bullet. As the theoretical presenter, I have made a mental note to discuss its importance in my opening remarks. Seven bullets on one slide is too many, anyway.

- The point of the "consumer driven" bullet is that the phrase is being redefined. The quote marks around the words imply that, so no other words are needed. If I were the presenter, the quotes would be all the reminder I would need about this topic.

- The final bullet has been promoted to title. If I were the content creator, I could see planning the entire presentation around that catchy phrase. Shoot, if the company were looking for a

When the Words Must Display

We know of several organizations that require that bullets be fleshed out into complete thoughts and displayed for the audience. (One company actually suffered through litigation based on the charge that it did not divulge visually specific information to an audience of shareholders...oy vey.)

As the content creator in this situation, you might not have a choice about how bloated your bullets become, but you do have a choice about when they take on this bloat. Using your newly-honed three-word skills, create the best bullet slide you know how. Then before the presenter advances to the next idea, have your three-word slide fade into the more verbose slide. Now the slide acts as a summary of the ideas just presented, and your organization's requirement for verbosity is satisfied.

This works even if the verbose slide displays word-for-word what the presenter just said. The axiom about being an idiot for reciting a slide only applies if the slide is present while you are reciting it. If the words appear afterward, you're not an idiot, you're omniscient.

marketing catch phrase, this could be it! At a minimum, it serves well as the frame for this slide.

It took four passes and over 45 minutes to finish the revision. Mark Twain would have been proud...

In the case of bullets, less is so much more. Playing the three-word game is one of the best devices to get you to less.

Brief bullets, stupid bullets...what's the difference?

In Chapter 6, we wrote about how ill-conceived bullets could keep you from fleshing out your ideas. Actually, we wrote that they could make you stupid. How is the three-word game different? This is a legitimate question and detractors of this strategy would argue that silly and evasive bullets offer no guarantee that an important idea will be shared, while a verbose bullet at least promises that the idea will be made public.

I don't have anything to say to refute this argument—the risk definitely exists that subtle bullets could ultimately neglect an idea if the presenter doesn't share his or her thoughts adequately. This, of course, would be the same result if there were no slides at all, and that ultimately is where the argument should head:

> **Would the presentation be effective without any slides at all?**

Hopefully, you can answer yes to that question.

> **Would the presence of slides make it better?**

And we want you to be able to answer yes to that one, too. If you start from the premise that *you* are the primary conduit of information exchange, you get off on the right foot. From there, ask yourself how your slides can help you deliver the message. From this perspective, it's hard not to conclude that slides that have been *three-worded* will support the presentation of ideas better than ones that drone on.

The War Against "On Click"

There is a battle of wills being fought in the boardrooms and in the trenches where America creates its presentation content. The controversy has raged on for the past five years and numerous articles and scathing editorials have been written about the bitter battle. We refer, of course, to the issue of bullet advancement: Do you display them all at once or click by click?

I come down on a particular side of this issue and I'm pleased to report that my side is winning: advancing one by one through bullets is losing favor, and in this section, I will tell you why the all-at-once choice is the better approach to take and how to best incorporate it.

We understand the appeal for advancing slides "on click." It could make pacing easier, it provides good breadcrumbs, and if you are new to using a wireless remote, it gives you extra opportunity to play with your cool new toy. But there are three significant downsides to this approach that you must take into account:

Loss of context

When you reveal ideas one by one, you ask the audience to absorb each piece of information by itself, and this often results in less-than-total understanding of the concept you are trying to share. As the presenter, you understand the connection between Bullets 1 and 3, but when you remove the forest and only show the trees, one by one, the audience doesn't get the same chance to connect the ideas.

Where's the end?

When you advance bullets one by one, you might lose the forest yourself! You increase the chances that you will forget which bullet is the last one and then have to do the advance-oops-sorry-go-back shuffle. Not the end of the world, but a needless disruption of your flow.

How dare you!

Most important, when you spoon-feed information to your audience, you could actually be insulting them. Some of your audience members could infer from this that you lack confidence in their ability to follow along. They see it as commentary on their intelligence. In the polls that we have taken, about one in 15 have reacted this way. If you're speaking to a room of 100, you would be offending six people just by the way you have created your bullet slides.

Figure 7.3 on the next page represents the nadir of this design approach—dimming bullets after you're done with them. This is downright condescending and will be felt on a conscious or subconscious level by more than just one in 15. Not only do you imply to your audience that they are not worthy of seeing what you have to say next, but that they need to be told when to stop paying attention to the last point.

You didn't mean any of that. You were just trying to be helpful. Or perhaps you just learned how to do all that stuff with the Custom

Figure 7.3
"You're not smart enough to keep up with me, so I will employ Sesame Street-type measures to help you."

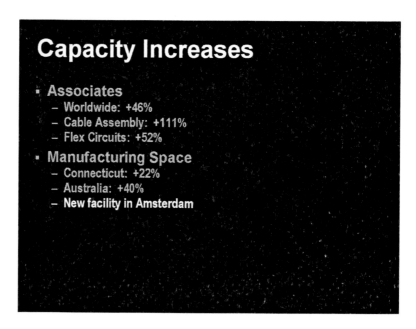

Animation task pane and you wanted to try it out. How did this get so out of hand?

Life is Too Short

Bullets on slides are just not worth this kind of trouble. Everyone's life is made easier when you display your bullets all at once and then speak to them. You insult nobody and you eliminate the risk that you might lose your own place. You make your life easier as the presenter, too—one click and you're there.

Nay-sayers will argue that audience members will run ahead and stop listening to you. Get real. How far ahead can they go? Do you have 22 bullets on the slide? I know presenters who refrain from distributing their handouts for this reason, and that is a legitimate point of view. But if your audience is having trouble paying attention to you, don't blame your bullets.

When you liberate your bullets in this way, you also get the opportunity to practice one of my favorite animation techniques for text blocks: the faded cascade:

1. Select the bullet placeholder and apply a fade for an entrance. Set Start to With Previous and Speed to Fast.

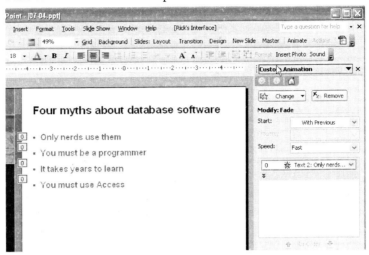

2. Click the downward-pointing arrows to expand the animated elements into their individual bullets, and if necessary, right-click on one of them and choose Show Advanced Timeline.

Not seeing the downward arrows? Your text is probably in a text box instead of a placeholder. But you can still use this method. Right click the animation and select Effect Options. Click the Text Animation Tab. Use the drop-down arrow to change the Group Text option to By 1st Level Paragraph, then click OK. Now you should see the arrows and be able to proceed.

3. Click and drag the second bullets' duration (its orange

bar) to the right by .2 seconds.

4. Drag each subsequent bullet to the right an additional .2 seconds.

5. Press Shift+F5 to play the current slide and witness your masterpiece.

Open 07-04.ppt from the betterppt.com web site to see the effect.

This is one of the most elegant treatments of text animation that we know. It is softer than a standard fade and very pleasing to the eye. It has only one drawback: Because it involves different animations to the same level of bullets, it cannot be programmed onto a slide master; it can only be created on content slides. Therefore, I do not employ this technique when I am looking to automate a 300-slide presentation.

The Art of Compromise

There will be occasions when you are either compelled by specific circumstances or by certain people (who sign your paycheck) to either advance bullets one by one or do the dreaded dim thing. And to be fair, we can think of situations in which it is appropriate to advance bullet by bullet or to highlight the specific idea that is being discussed. Here are a couple of recommended strategies for those times.

Is this the last bullet on your slide??

If you are compelled to display bullets one by one, here is a trick that will insure against your inadvertently advancing beyond the last bullet and switching to the next slide before you wanted to.

1. Open the slide in question and make note of its background color. In our example, it is a blue gradient.

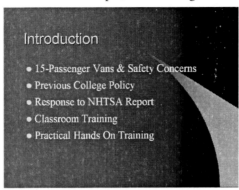

2. Create a thin rule in an out-of-the-way place, close to the color of the background. We placed ours along the bottom of the slide and filling it with a blue that is a bit lighter than the background.

3. Animate it, using the generic Appear for the type and After Previous for the Start. Make sure it is at the bottom of the animation sequence.

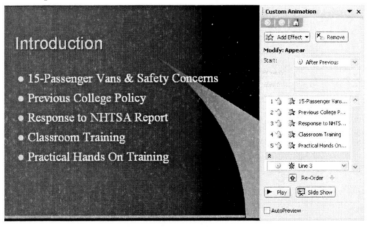

Download 07-05.ppt to see this tactic in action.

Now when you show this slide, that thin rule will inconspicuously appear immediately after the last bullet appears. You know that your bullets for that slide have all displayed and you can focus on your ideas, without having to wonder if you dare click your remote one more time. It's an opportunity to reduce by one the things a presenter has to think about while in front of an audience.

Your audience probably won't notice your end-of-slide cue, but it's not a problem if they do. In fact, I know presenters who display a prominent "End of Slide" text box on their slide, in full view of everyone, after the last element appears. I don't think there is any problem at all allowing your audience to see the plumbing in your PowerPoint house. That just shows that you have given this some thought and are striving to create a smooth experience for everyone.

You are here

Should it become necessary to highlight the particular bullet you are speaking on, there are right ways and wrong ways to do it.

- Dimming everything except that bullet is the wrong way.

- Showing everything and highlighting the current one is the right way.

Download 07-06.ppt to see this effect in action.

The following example assumes that you need to show a lengthy list and discuss many of the points on that list. Our slide has 20 items on it, so we used the side-by-side layout, requiring that the following steps be performed twice.

1. Animate your bullets however you normally do. We have chosen to create a fade on the master slide, set Very Fast, After Previous.

2. On the slide, select the bullet placeholder and add the Change Font Color emphasis. Pick a color close to the font color. With our white text on a dark background, we chose yellow.

3. From the Effects dialog box (right-click on the object in the Animation task pane to get there), set the After Animation to be the original color of the bullets.

To summarize, there are two animations applied to the text. The first one is a conventional fade that brings all of the bullets in at once. The second animation, set On Click, changes the color of each bullet with each click of the mouse or remote. And while each click changes a bullet's color, it also sets the previous bullet's color back to its original.

I vastly prefer this to dimming or spoon-feeding the text. This double-animation technique gets all of the text out there at once and then allows you to highlight each one without being condescending.

We spent many minutes coming up with an example that we think justifies this type of treatment, and it might be several months before we use it again. Please do not use this technique without cause!

Chapter 8

Be the Master of Your Own Slide

The name of this chapter can be interpreted two ways: One, to be so adept at the mechanics of slide creation that you can pump them out in record time; two, to be smart and use the built-in tools that automate slide formatting.

We accept either interpretation.

This chapter focuses on the potentially dramatic control you can wield over your work by using the Slide Master engine.

It is also the first chapter requiring that we depart from our practice of *versionlessness*. Those still using PowerPoint from Office 2000 will suffer Version Envy through our discussion of slide masters, and those exploring Office 2007 will find this component to be entirely rewritten.

A Semantic of Questions

Wait, shouldn't that be "A Question of Semantics?" Yes, it should, just like Microsoft should have chosen between calling them *slide masters* and referring to the *master slide*. It is one of several instances of lazy language on the part of the program developers, which inhibits total understanding of this otherwise fine tool. So let's begin with a definition of terms, courtesy of PowerPoint's on-line Help:

Slide Master
An element of the design template that stores information about the template, including: font styles, placeholders, sizes, positions, background design, and color schemes.

Master Slide
See Slide Master.

Design Template
A file that contains: the styles in a presentation, including the type and size of bullets and fonts; placeholder sizes and positions; background design and fill color schemes.

Title Master
Contains placeholders for a title, subtitle, and headers and footers.

◆

These definitions seem perfectly fine on their face, until you dive into the program. At that point, you will discover:

- Slide masters do not live just in the design template; they are a part of every PowerPoint file created.

- The program interface refers to individual slide masters as templates.

- The Title master is not a master onto itself but part of a set of masters.

- The most intuitive maneuver for applying a specific master to a particular slide will actually apply that master to every slide in your presentation.

Once you overcome these cognitive hurdles, working with slide masters is not difficult. But we know from surveying hundreds of content creators that these hurdles keep many from becoming one with slide masters. Therefore, much of the focus of this chapter will be to help you overcome the gotchas.

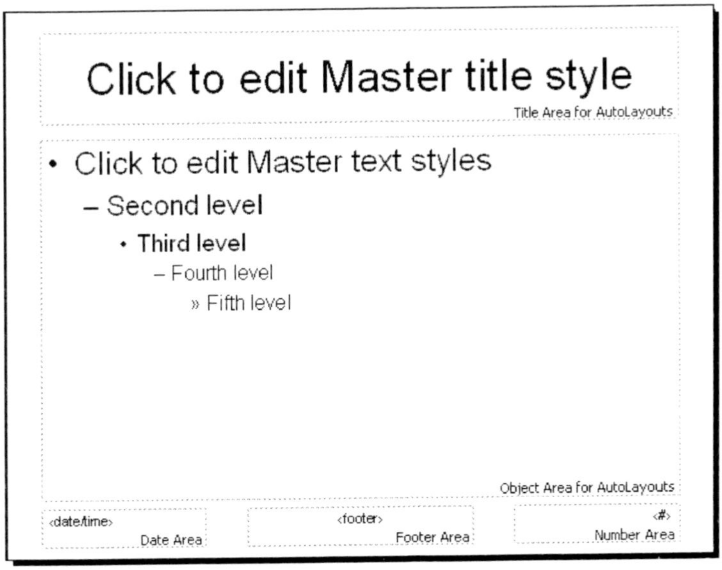

Figure 8.1
The slide master's
first impression is not
much different than
that of a standard
slide.

Understanding the Slide Master

At its core, the slide master is a global control: elements that you place on it will be present on the individual slides of your presentation. Similarly, formatting that you apply to those elements will affect the look and behavior of individual slides.

Object creation and formatting are carried out the same on a slide master as on a regular slide, so half the battle is in finding your way:

View | Master | Slide Master

That takes you to the relatively simple interface shown here in Figure 8.1. With very few exceptions, everything you can do on a normal slide can also be done here:

- Format titles and bullets

- Choose a background

- Add photos

- Create an animation scheme

Does my interface look different than yours? That's because mine has been customized to suit my every whim—see Chapter 17 to learn how you can do it, too.

The one significant difference in behavior is a friendly one: It's much easier to format the placeholders. Local text formatting inside a placeholder has no meaning on a slide master — you can't drag across two or three words of the sample text ("Click to edit Master text styles") and make any meaningful changes to them. Those words get replaced by the actual content on your slides so nothing that you do to individually selected words matters.

Therefore, any formatting you do inside a placeholder is done to the entire level that is selected. Plant your cursor anywhere and Power-Point assumes you are formatting the level, not a word on that line. In fact, when you first plant your cursor, you'll notice that the entire level is initially selected.

So a single click is all you need to tell PowerPoint what to change.

The Title Master

The first point of confusion that befalls users is the direction that appears in big letters:

> **Click to edit Master title style**

They see the word "title" in Figure 8.1 and think that this has to do with their title slide. It doesn't. Most slide formats include a title—this placeholder controls the appearance and function of the title on any slide in the presentation that uses this slide master.

In order to create a specific design for the title slide(s) in your presentation, you would create a "title master," easily achieved by right-clicking on the slide thumbnail and clicking New Title Master.

Not so fast, though. The key to creating your title master is not the how, but the *when*. When title masters are born, they inherit the attributes of the slide master, but as they grow up, they have lives of their own. Most changes made to the slide master do not affect the title master, and vice-versa.

We hope that you seek an integrated design throughout your presentation, both title and content slides. To accomplish that, your two masters would share many attributes, such as background, color scheme, font choice, etc. If you were to create your title master from the presentation in Figure 8.1, it would look just as plain as the slide master does.

Figure 8.2 shows a more refined design, the one that we used as the standard template for all presentations given at PowerPoint Live 2006. This is the right time to create the title master, which, as you can see by its thumbnail, picks up all of the elements designed into the slide master.

Figure 8.2

Wait until you have finished designing the major elements of your slide master before creating your title master—it will deliver you from much repetition.

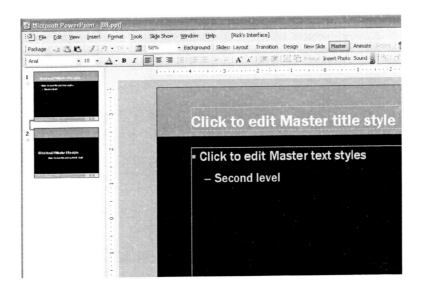

Deb Shenenberg of Scottsdale AZ designed this template and submitted it to the annual PowerPoint Live Design Contest. As the winning entry, Deb won a free pass to the conference. To enter the contest, visit www.PowerPointLive.com.

There is one attribute that is linked between the two masters...sort of. If you format the Master Title style in the slide master, that change will be reflected in the title master. The reverse is not true, however, and this bedevils unsuspecting users who see their titles change seemingly randomly. So again, go as far as you can with your slide master design before creating the title master.

Creating Multiple Masters

At this point, have you created one master or two? Simple question...complicated answer. In the thumbnails of Figure 8.2, there are gray connector lines linking the two slides. That is your cue that these two masters are joined at the virtual hip. It is better to think of them as a single set of masters. Hover the mouse over either one and you will see that they are named the same (Default Design).

Since PowerPoint XP (the one previous to PowerPoint 2003), ambitious users can create additional sets of masters, proving invaluable for those seeking maximum flexibility through minimal effort. We'll walk through the classic example right now: the creation of a "print master," to facilitate the printing of a presentation. (While it is fine for projected presentations to be white text on black, it is far better for printed presentations to be black text on white.)

Part Two: The Solution

Figure 8.3
If you want a new master to look like an existing one, don't use the New Title Master command. That will get you a plain slide and buy you a lot of extra work.

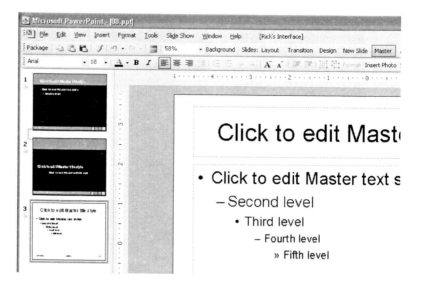

Users of PowerPoint 2000 cannot create multiple master styles, while users of PowerPoint 2007 can create so much more. They can create "themes"—see the discussion later in this chapter.

If you were to create the second master according to conventional instructions, you would not be a happy camper. Figure 8.3 shows the result of right-clicking in the thumbnail area and choosing New Slide Master: a plain vanilla master with none of your design elements. Instead, do this:

1. Select one of your master thumbnails and copy and paste it (Ctrl+C and Ctrl+V), or press Ctrl+D to duplicate it.

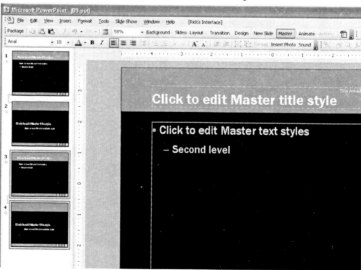

2. Individually select the new title master and delete it.

3. On the new slide master, select the entire master text style place-holder. In other words, don't just drop your cursor onto one of the text levels; select the boundary for all of the text levels. The easiest way to accomplish this is to press and hold Shift while you click the text. If your cursor is already planted in the text, press Esc to change the selection to the placeholder.

4. Set the text to black. It will promptly disappear against the black background.

5. Change the slide background to white, being careful to click Apply, and not Apply to All, which in this case would change the background for all masters.

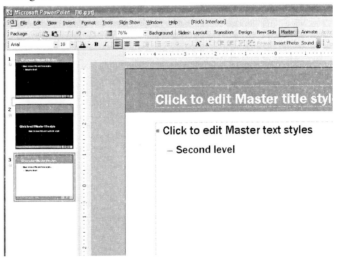

6. Right-click the new master thumbnail and choose New Title Master, at which point the only tweak that is needed is to set the title to black and perhaps center it in its placeholder.

7. Right-click either new master thumbnail, choose Rename Master, and call it Print.

You now have a set of masters tuned for printing out your presentation. How do you use this second set of masters?

1. Go to View | Normal view to leave Master view and return to Normal view.

2. Go to Format | Slide Design to invoke the Design task pane.

3. From the section entitled "Apply a design template used in this presentation," right-click your new slide master, entitled Print

and choose Apply to All Slides.

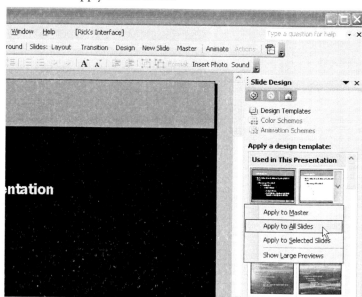

This change is instantaneous across every slide in your presentation: they all immediately take on the look of the Print master.

Changing out an entire presentation is simple; ironically, applying a new slide master to just one or two slides is not as easy. For reasons known only to the developers, the default action when you click on a new master in the Slide Design task pane is to apply it to *every* slide in the presentation. If you aren't aware of this quirk, it could have a negative impact on your career. To apply a slide master only to the selected slide, you must right-click the master (or click the downward-pointing arrow) and choose Apply to Selected Slide.

Mixing and Matching

There are countless examples of opportunities to create additional sets of slide masters. I have colleagues and clients who have designed "quote masters," a slide on which they display quotations, section divider slides, slide masters that simply display "Any Questions?", and ones that prominently display contact information and company URL.

If you download columbus.ppt from the betterppt.com web site, you will see an example of how Christopher Columbus might have made use of multiple slide masters when trying to get funding from the Queen for his big voyage. There are four sets of masters in that file:

Standard: Conventional design with basic Wipe Right applied to the bullets.

Print: Designed specifically for printouts.

Self-Running Presentation: Columbus isn't certain that he will be able to get an audience with the Queen in person, so he designed a set of masters in case he needs to, um, email his presentation to her. This set offers a bit more animation (without a live presenter, the slides need to work a bit harder) and includes prompts for when to advance to the next slide.

Just the Facts: The Queen is a very busy lady who doesn't have time for things to spin, fly, wipe, or even fade. This set of masters displays each slide with no motion at all.

We noted earlier the unfortunate choice to make the default action affect every slide instead of just the current one. The other obtuse aspect of slide masters is the developers' decision to refer to them as "design templates" in the Slide Design task pane. A template file lives on a different rung of the conceptual ladder from a slide master (slide masters are a part of every presentation file; a template *is* a presentation file). Granted, you can import the slide design from a template or from a different presentation file in the same way that you swap out a slide master. Nonetheless, the decision to refer to a slide master as a template has served to confuse more than enlighten.

▼ There are two other types of masters in PowerPoint: the Handout master and the Notes master, both of which we plead guilty to ignoring. If you print handouts regularly, it is worth your taking the time to explore the ways in which the standard layouts for handouts can be customized.

Understanding Templates

Apologies in advance if this section comes off as glib or flippant.

> **To create a template,**
> **rename the extension to .pot.**

That, ladies and gentlemen, is the entire difference between a regular presentation file and a template in versions 2003 and earlier. You can turn any presentation file into a template by changing its extension. When you double-click a .pot file, Windows does not open it directly; instead, it imports the content into a new, untitled, unsaved presentation.

If you wanted to directly edit a template file, use the Open command within PowerPoint and change the Files of Type filter to Design Templates.

Any PowerPoint file, regardless of its extension, can be used as a template to spawn other presentations. All of the choices are available from the Slide Design task pane:

- Slide masters within the current presentation

- Presentation templates that live on your hard drive, either because you created them or because they were placed there during installation.

- Templates that you can download from the Microsoft Office web site.

- And via the Browse button, any presentation file—.ppt or .pot extension—that you can find within your network of computers.

The New Horizon of Version 2007

Without question, one of the areas that sees the most evolution in the current version of PowerPoint is the handling of masters. To those who have become fluent with the capabilities and deficiencies of slide masters, the new version's offerings will be impossible to ignore.

Figure 8.5
This layout is very attractive, but prior to version 2007, not very customizable.

The Politics of Philanthropy

Being pragmatic doesn't make you selfish

Dr. Martin Zackheim
Professor of Humanities
Darmouth University

Figure 8.6

With version 2007's custom placeholders, you gain control and flexibility.

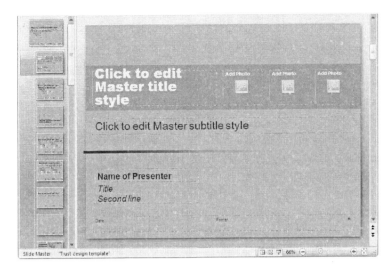

Veteran users cite two long-standing weaknesses with slide masters—not enough placeholders on a layout and not enough layouts—and they are most easily described with scenarios.

Let's say you have created a terrific title master for a symposium that will include 70 presenters across four days. Figure 8.5 shows the title slide for one of the presentations. It is a very clean, professional look with an eye toward flexibility: each presenter fills in his or her name and title, and can substitute in three photos of choice to the right of the title.

Flexibility is fine, unless you are the organizer trying to maintain consistency across 100 presentations. What are the chances that one, two, or 30 presenters won't set his name in 36 pt., or the odds that she won't mangle the placement of those photos?

These are elements that really belong on the slide master—after all, they are designed to be placeholders, into which presenters place their own content. But PowerPoint has never offered these types of controls; any photos or text that you place outside of the two placeholders (title and subtitle for title masters, title and text for slide masters) become permanent. Therefore, you would have to place these elements on the slides themselves, putting them at risk of being mangled by inexperienced users or forgotten if extra title slides are called for deeper into a presentation.

Version 2007 addresses this issue with custom placeholders, allowing you to identify three photos on the title slide, each at just the right size and location, and text boxes for the speaker's name and position. Figure 8.6 shows how you would create the title master with these placeholders, using the richer controls of version 2007.

At the risk of insult, I want to reiterate the difference here between the versions. With Version 2003 and earlier, you can place a string of text on your title master that reads "Name of Presenter," as you see in Figure 8.6. And you can drop three photos adjacent to the title placeholder. But when you returned to Normal view and went to a title slide, you would see "Name of Presenter," on the slide, and you wouldn't be able to edit it!

As Figure 8.7 shows, in PowerPoint 2007 the text in a placeholder functions as instructions to the person building the slide. The content you type in the placeholder on the master slide is replaced when you edit the actual slide.

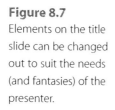

Download 08-07.pptx and open with Version 2007 to see how the new placeholders operate.

The second weakness with slide masters prior to version 2007 is how incapable they are of controlling content on anything other than standard-issue bullet slides. The text placeholders do influence text formatting on charts and graphs, but the relationship is bizarre and virtually impossible to understand. This is one of many vestiges of a software application that did not anticipate users doing much beyond creating bullet slides.

In version 2007, you create custom slide layouts within each slide master, one for each type of slide you anticipate using. Charts could have their own layouts and a specific size for text, double-column bullets, photo spreads, hybrid slides, anything.

Figure 8.8 gives you a taste: This layout allows you to customize the caption text for a photo, chart, or graph. But let's back up and give

Figure 8.7
Elements on the title slide can be changed out to suit the needs (and fantasies) of the presenter.

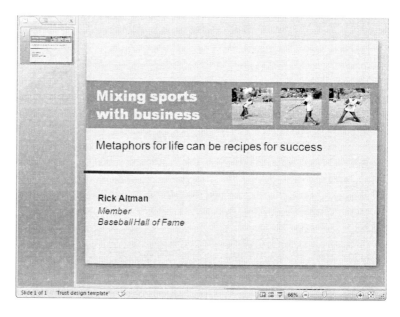

Figure 8.8
The "Content With Caption" Layout is one of 12 slide masters included in the templates that ship with PowerPoint 2007.

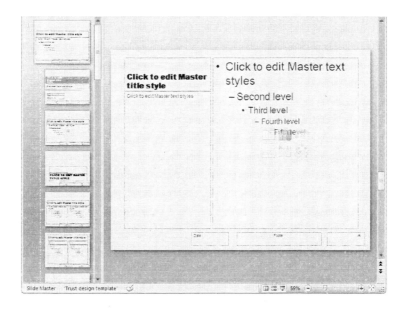

the new version brownie points for even acknowledging in the first place that you might want to have a caption for your graphic. No previous version of PowerPoint accommodated that.

PowerPoint 2007 also addresses the conceptual disconnect between slide masters and templates by adding a layer called a theme. A theme consists of backgrounds, color schemes, typeface selections, and design motifs. The theme is a better paradigm than the template and is more usable, as you can distribute it to Word and Excel users as easily as to other PowerPoint users. Here is a new palette of color schemes, any number of which can be included in a theme.

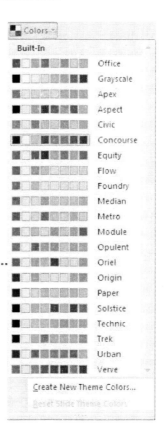

Themes should replace templates altogether, but legacy considerations mandated the continuation of the now-simplistic template. If you are an earnest user of slide masters and

Part Two: The Solution

begin using PowerPoint 2007, chances are good you will dump templates in favor of themes.

Master Miscellany

With any version later than 2000, the idea of creating more than one set of masters within your presentation file takes you to a new plateau of productivity and it is worth the investment of time and creative effort to try to anticipate your future needs and build masters that would address them.

- How many ways do you present your company logo?

- Do you regularly create segue slides between sections or topics? Would you rather not simply reuse the title slide layout?

- Do you like to design your own "blank" slide?

- Do you create nice watermarked backgrounds but still regularly need to work with a flat background?

These are a few of the scenarios that are addressed with the creation of more than one set of slide masters in a presentation. Start to take advantage of them and you officially graduate from the School of the First 15 Minutes.

Chapter 9

Creating Custom Shows

If you were to poll 20 experts in PowerPoint usage, it is likely that exactly none of them would list the topic of this chapter as among the most vital. And that is the beauty of writing a book that is designed to be uneven: I can indulge in the arcane and burrow into the obscure, and there's nothing you can do about it!

Of course, you could always just skip this chapter. Go ahead...I dare you to not read this chapter. I double-dog dare you to just jump right over it. See, now you're stuck, you have to read it. Good thing, too, because while doing all of that burrowing, I have unearthed a topic that is one of PowerPoint's unsung heroes.

You might go weeks at a time without using it. You might only use it in specific situations. But the fluent practitioners of their craft recognize the creation of the custom show as one of the jewels that combines flexibility with economy of effort.

Many Shows, One File

At its core, the Custom Show engine is a means by which you can create a superset of a presentation: you can develop all of the slides that you anticipate that you might *ever* use on a given topic, and then slice and dice it for any given presentation.

Creating a custom show is not unlike hiding a group of slides, but it is more flexible: while you can only hide/unhide one group of slides at a time, you can create many custom shows.

1. Go to Slide Show | Custom Shows, click New, and devise a name for your custom show.

2. From the list on the left of every slide in the current file, double-click the ones you want to include in the custom show.

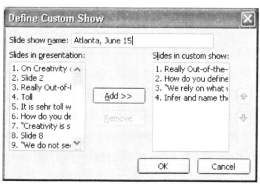

3. Click OK and then Close.

4. To use a custom show, go to Slide Show | Set Up Show.

5. In the Show Slides section, click Custom Show and highlight the name of the show you created in the drop-down list.

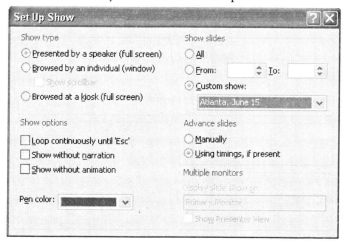

The next time you show this presentation, only the slides in the custom show will display.

Less Flotsam, Better Focus

This beats the heck out of giving a presentation that is full of slides that you know you won't get to, yet that happens thousands of time every day. Nothing like motoring through two dozen slides in five seconds to take your focus away from your delivery.

As bad as that sounds, it's better than what *Presentations* magazine recommended several years ago: for each type of presentation you might give, save the PowerPoint file under a different name and then remove the slides you don't want.

Talk about flotsam. What happens when it's time to update the main content? How many versions of the presentation file will you have to open and change? Granted, tailoring a presentation for a particular client or situation is standard procedure, but it should be done from a single slide deck that you clearly recognize as the most current and up-to-date version of your presentation. That can't happen if you have several different versions, each claiming to function as a base presentation or a template.

And let's be clear here that it really doesn't matter if your template is an actual template file, with a .pot extension, or a plain old .ppt file. As we discussed last chapter, there is no real difference between them. The best argument for using a .pot file is the insurance against your inadvertently overwriting the file because you forgot to perform a Save As. The argument against: it's not very easy to make changes to it when you really want to.

But we don't care on which side of that fence you choose to live: having all of your content in one file is the important tonic here, and knowing about custom shows is the straw that stirs that drink.

Case Study

You might know one of my clients: his name is Albert Einstein. Arden Bercovitz does a very good Einstein and he has been touring the country delivering uplifting and motivating lectures as the brilliant scientist/philosopher.

He has appeared at both CorelWorld and PowerPoint Live, but before presenting to a group of presentation pros at PPTLive, he knew that his slides needed an overhaul. He is not a slave to bullets

Figure 9.2
Albert Einstein would probably have designed slides like this back in his day, but the modern-day Einstein wanted a more professional look.

and speaks to his visuals like a pro. But as you can see from his slide master in Figure 9.2, he has not benefited from working with a graphic designer.

De-cluttering his slides and cleaning up his look was not difficult, and Figure 9.3 shows the basic makeover that I performed for him. Just two masters—one for basic content and one for quotes from the good doctor, with an image of him faded into the background. You'll notice that the standard slide master, the first thumbnail, has no bullet—just centered text.

The bigger challenge was accommodating all of his ideas and the creative way he expressed them. The side-by-side photos of Mona Lisa and Mr. Spock...the coining of "Schlimmbe" (improvements that make things worse), and some great quotes ("The only sure way to avoid mistakes is to have no new ideas.").

I recommended to Arden that he prepare for a presentation by acting out the role of Jim Phelps in Mission: Impossible. The baby boomers among our readers might remember the classic opening to the television show, right after the tape self-destructed in five seconds. Jim would sit at his coffee table and prepare his IM force. He would browse through the dossiers of several secret agents, figuring out the best match for the specific impossible task ahead. He would invariably pick the same people—television budgets for casting being what they were in the 1960s—but the impression created was that he hand-picked just the right players for the team he needed to have.

Figure 9.3
No reason Albert shouldn't benefit from a cleaner, more unified look.

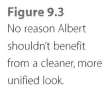
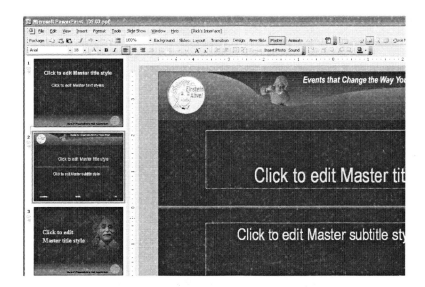

Arden liked that analogy but was quick to point out that he might change his mind about which slides to use right up to the morning of a keynote. He didn't want to be locked into a specific set of slides.

This has custom show written all over it. As you can see from Figure 9.4, Arden's slide deck is tremendously vast. Just look at the scroll bar along the right edge for an idea of how many slides live in his template.

From here, he picks the slides that he chooses to use on a given day. Instead of Jim Phelps' coffee table, he uses the Custom Show dialog box. At any time, according to circumstance or whimsy, he can modify the custom show to add or remove slides.

Figure 9.4
One presentation file...a lifetime of slides...

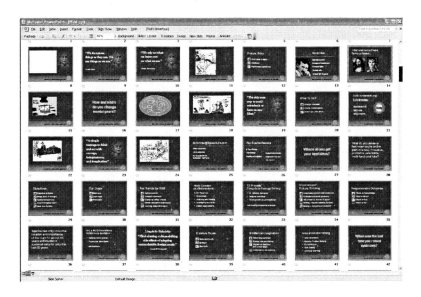

Part Two: The Solution

Figure 9.5

If you have a handful of typical presentations you give, you can create generic custom shows to jump-start the process.

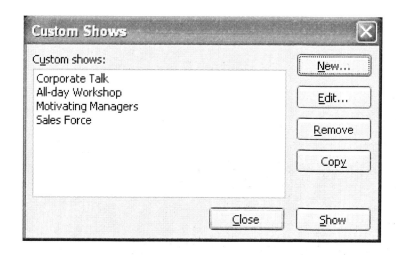

Arden could go one step further and build standard shows into his template. As Figure 9.5 illustrates, if his lectures fall into general categories, he can build custom shows for those categories that give him an excellent starting point to building a particular presentation.

Just so we're clear, I'm not suggesting that Arden, or you, work off of the same file for every presentation. You will surely be adding specific content that suits the client or the situation; hence, you will invariably be saving your template file under a specific name and customizing it from there.

The key is what spawns this custom file, and the more complete your template, the better your starting point. When you get comfortable with custom shows, you can begin to think like Jim Phelps or the head coach or manager of your favorite team (warning, runaway sports analogy ahead). You have your players and for each game, you assemble the best team you can. Your starting players are in your custom show; the rest are on your bench, ready to see action at a moment's notice.

May your players all be all-stars and may your team win the championship. Groan...

Chapter 10

The Art of Transparency

The first thing to be said about this topic is that it's a fake. Software programs that can create transparent effects are doing something that is fundamentally impossible in the two-dimensional world of computing. Only in the real world can you see through objects; anytime it happens on a computer screen, it's an illusion.

But oh, what a clever lie these programs tell when they provide the means to create transparent effects. And oh, how useful it can be toward creating dramatic designs and solving problems. In this chapter, we'll explore both the dramatic and the pragmatic elements of transparency. In the process, we'll be journeying outside the software.

Through the Looking Glass

PowerPoint versions 2003 and earlier have simple transparency built into the program, as all of its vector shapes (rectangles, ellipses, triangles, etc., but not standard text) can be made to be see-through, provided they are closed shapes. Again, this is just a clever fake: PowerPoint studies the object underneath the transparent shape and whips up an on-the-fly bitmap representation of what the object would look like were there really a shape atop it of a certain color and percentage of opacity.

Unlike with drawing programs, where it's only a worthwhile effect if it can print properly, your burden as a presentation designer is friendlier: if it looks good on screen, you're golden.

Figure 10.1
This photo is too strong to serve as a background. It overpowers the text placed on top of it.

Rescuing background images

Figure 10.1 revisits the dilemma we spelled out in Chapter 4, Bitter Backgrounds, of using photos that are too bright, too big, too colorful, too full of contrast. Those are normally good qualities for a photo to have, but not when you are trying to use it as a background. Then you want it to be more subdued.

The simplest of maneuvers can do wonders for this slide. Watch:

1. Draw a rectangle over the entire slide and color it a deep navy blue.

2. Using the layering commands, place the rectangle behind the text but in front of the photo.

3. Right-click the rectangle and choose Format AutoShape.

4. Drag the Transparency slider to the right, clicking Preview to survey various values. At 10%, you can just barely see the photo.

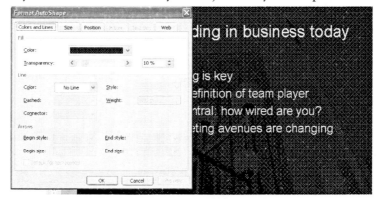

5. Click OK when you have found a satisfactory value. Figure 10.3 shows how a 15% transparency makes the text on the slide perfectly readable.

Figure 10.3
A transparent rectangle draped over the photo reduces its contrast and makes it more suitable as a background.

Download 10-03.ppt from betterppt.com to see how this is done.

This simple technique has significant implications so I want us to stay here for a couple of paragraphs. Once you know how to tint back a photo, you make it possible to use practically any photo as a background. As we discussed in Chapter 4, overly loud backgrounds are among the most annoying qualities in all of PowerPointdom. With one rectangle, you can completely eliminate this source of annoyance.

In the steps above, I used navy blue because it matched the predominant color of the photo. I could also have used black (dramatic), white (for a washout effect, to be used with dark text), brown (urban), green (environmental)...in each case when you drape a color over the photo you mute all of its colors and reduce its contrast, making it a suitable candidate for a background image.

 Tinting of photos is one of many new capabilities offered in version 2007, allowing you to just alter the photo directly. Stay tuned...

Half transparent, half opaque

There are times when sinking a photo into the background is exactly what you want and other times when a strong photo needs to remain prominent. In the latter case, you can solve major design challenges by adopting the transparent shape strategy.

Figure 10.4 shows one possible implementation, as the text has been confined to one corner and the transparent rectangle shrunk down to fit in that space. This kind of integration of text and image is usually

Figure 10.4
This transparency blends well with the photo, creating a unified look.

the domain of design professionals, so be prepared to get lots of props when you roll out slides like this.

When taking an object all the way to the edge of the slide, it pays to actually go one click beyond the slide boundary. Some older projectors and/or video cards might be a pixel off in their display of vector objects and could create an annoying line of color at the edge. This is the equivalent of a printer's registration error, and is corrected the same way as with a job for press: by bleeding the image over the edge.

All of Figure 10.4 can be programmed into the slide master: the full-screen photo, the transparent rectangle, the title contained within that small space, and the bullets underneath them. Prepare to be

Figure 10.5
A gradient transparency is nice for blending objects into a background.

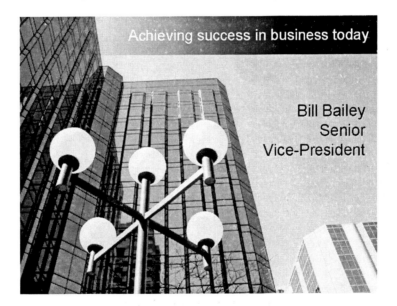

heavy-handed with content editing, as many standard-length titles would be too long and you'd be hard-pressed to fit more than four bullets into that space. Hmm, another benefit to this design...

Figure 10.5 shows the use of a gradient transparency—a level of transparency that is gradually changing. There are three things worth noting here:

- I did not create a rectangle to be placed behind the text; instead, I used the text placeholder itself. It can accept a fill pattern and be fitted with transparency, just like any other Power-Point shape. From the Format AutoShape dialog, you can set margins for the placeholder and determine where the text is to be situated within the space.

▪ You create a gradient transparency by choosing to blend from one color to the same color, varying the transparency value for each.

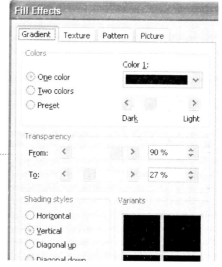

I could not reconcile the jarring intrusion of the flagpole stretching into the sky, so I removed it. As this is a stock photo to which I purchased unrestricted usage rights, I am at liberty to modify it any way I deem fit, which in this case was via the Clone tool of my image-editing software.

Applying Transparency to Photos

So far, this chapter has focused on applying transparency to simple shapes and placing them atop photos and images. The ante gets upped when we talk about applying transparency directly to the

Figure 10.7
This nice effect was created in...
PowerPoint?

photo. This is not simple stuff, but it's worth the effort as the effects you can create are potentially breathtaking.

If I told you that one of the transparent effects in Figure 10.7 was created outside of PowerPoint, you could probably guess which effect, right? Go ahead, say which one before reading on. It's the cool photo of the golfer that was doctored up in an image-editing program, right? Wrong.

I gave you your clue in the third paragraph of this chapter: conventional text can not be made transparent in versions 2003 and earlier—only WordArt can, which is such a low-rent tool I don't even want to talk about it. The text was created in my preferred graphic drawing program, CorelDraw, where I applied a gradient transparency and exported it as a PNG file, the primary image format able to deliver information about sophisticated transparency.

But the photo...that was done in PowerPoint, and it presents an interesting cognitive challenge, for which you earn brownie points for even trying to solve. Let's review a few facts that we know:

- PowerPoint can apply transparency to vector shapes, provided they are closed.

- An ellipse is such a shape.

- Of the many fill patterns available, one of the options is to fill a shape with a photo.

- Irrespective of what's inside the ellipse, it can still be made transparent. Here's how in versions 2003 and earlier:

1. From the Fill Color drop-down in Format AutoShape, choose Fill Effects.

2. Click the Picture tab, and click Select Picture to find the photo.

3. Be sure to check Lock Picture Aspect Ratio to insure against distortion.

Download 10-07.ppt to see how we did this.

In this case, you are simply instructing PowerPoint to apply transparency to the ellipse. If the ellipse were filled with the color blue, you would see through to the photo underneath, which would be cast in a blue tint. In this case, the photo underneath is cast in a golfer tint. You're only seeing half of the ellipse because I hung the other half off of the slide. Open the file from the web site and you can see this for yourself.

Working with graphics software

As impressive as this is, the real power in these types of effects lies in your effective use of an external image-editing or graphic-drawing program. In the age of digital photography, fewer people understand the distinction between the two main types of graphics programs, vector and bitmap. They buy a camera and go on auto-pilot with whatever software is found on the accompanying CD. They tend to gloss over the fundamentals:

- Graphic-drawing software creates high-quality shapes based on mathematics (vectors). The most common programs in this space are Adobe Illustrator and CorelDraw.

- Image-editing software deals in pixels and turns its attention to photos, where you could literally change any one dot of an image. The most common program in this category is Adobe Photoshop, with Corel offering PhotoPaint and Paint Shop Pro.

Both categories of software have applications capable of creating transparent images that can be understood by PowerPoint. To get technical on you, these advanced programs create an *alpha channel*— an area of data reserved for transparent information.

What, you want more? Okay, computer monitors display color using the RGB model: all color is divided into percentages of red, green, and blue, and any software program that deals even in rudimentary color reserves three 8-bit channels for describing these three colors.

Professional-grade graphics and image-editing applications work with a fourth channel, the so-called alpha channel, which specifies how a pixel's color is to be merged with another pixel when the two are placed one atop the other. This is also referred to as a mask.

Before your eyes roll into the back of your head, know this: however these programs go about creating this type of magic, PowerPoint understands it. There aren't many file formats capable of delivering alpha channel information, and most of them are the formats native to the programs that deal in them:

- Adobe Photoshop (.psd)

- Adobe Illustrator (.ai)

- CorelDraw (.cdr)

- Corel PhotoPaint (.cpt) and Corel Paint Shop Pro (.psp)

PowerPoint cannot read any of these formats, but it does just fine with the PNG (Portable Network Graphics) format (pronounced *ping*). This is the one generic format capable of containing alpha channel information and all of the programs listed above can export to this format.

There is another format that supports transparency, the GIF format, but we recommend against its use. Its limited color palette (just 256 colors) and inability to make more than one color transparent makes it ill-suited for this type of work.

Going non-rectangular

When you import a standard image or graphic to PowerPoint, it comes in as a rectangle. A graphic has a *bounding box* that defines its size, and PowerPoint allocates that size and shape for the graphic, irrespective of whether it fills that size. This is why you might have been tripped up by the likes of Figure 10.9, where non-rectangular images import to PowerPoint with white space.

At the core of your challenge is the export of your non-rectangular and/or transparent images with the alpha channel information. This involves telling your software to pay attention to a portion of the

Part Two: The Solution

Figure 10.9
Nothing like a visible bounding box to ruin a nice design idea.

The most romantic
city in the world...

photo, not the entire one, and each program will differ in the terminology that it uses:

■ In Adobe Photoshop, you use the Marquee tool to define the shape and create a layer from the marquee (right-click | Layer via Cut). Then you use the Save As command, choosing PNG as the format.

■ In Corel PhotoPaint, you use the Mask tools to define the shape and then export to PNG, choosing Masked Area when prompted for Transparency.

■ In CorelDraw, you would either crop the photo to a certain shape or use the PowerClip command to place the photo within a closed shape. Then export to PNG, choosing Masked Area when prompted for Transparency.

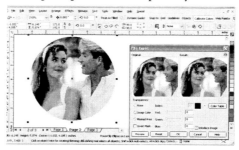

▼ Even though CorelDraw is a graphic drawing (vector) program, it is unusually adept at working with bitmap images, such as these photos.

Figure 10.11
When you tell an image to leave its background behind, PowerPoint listens.

From any of these programs (and from others), Figure 10.11 shows the happy result of importing that PNG file. All three programs were able to instruct PowerPoint to read the alpha channel information describing the shape of the image. No more bounding box!

This isn't exactly the holy grail here—you can produce the same effect by loading a photo into an ellipse or something more creative, as shown in Figure 10.12. Still, producing graphics without backgrounds is an important skill to have. Even though it requires a second application to make the PNG file, many veteran users prefer

Figure 10.12
Filling shapes with photos is useful to know, but creating PNGs with graphic software will take you further.

Figure 10.13
Complex transparency like this can be accurately described by the alpha channel.

doing that than wrestling with filled autoshapes, where setting the size and dimension can be frustrating.

Transparency on steroids

Understanding how the alpha channel works is not a requirement for taking advantage of it. In fact, I had to go to Wikipedia for the definition I gave earlier and I've been creating PNG files for over 10 years. But as you get some mileage under your belt, a new horizon of possibilities opens to you.

Figure 10.14
When PowerPoint imports a complex PNG file, it figures it all out.

▼ Download the PNG files created from each program, all in one .zip archive called couples.zip.

Programs that manipulate the alpha channel have developed inventive tools for controlling the function. Our favorite is CorelDraw for its blended support for both vector graphics and bitmap images and its ease of use. Figure 10.13 shows one of the choices in Draw's suite of interactive transparency tools, which can be applied to any object. This one is called "radial transparency," where a ring is defined from the inside (completely opaque) to the outside (completely transparent).

▼ Download 10.14.ppt to see the effect.

This is a complicated effect, in which the degree of transparency is constantly changing across the face of the image. Nonetheless, a PNG file can digest all of it. Figure 10.14 shows the potential drama created with these effects. Add a medium-speed fade entrance to it and you really have something extraordinary.

Figure 10.15
A few of the many built-in effects available in version 2007 that can be applied to imported photos...

Better Graphics with Version 2007

When we first looked at the new version of PowerPoint, we wondered if we had to throw out this whole chapter and rewrite it, so pervasive are the changes made to the controls for imported photos.

Thankfully, we don't have to do that; in fact, in some ways, it's just the opposite (more on that soon). But first, let's be candid that the photo manipulation that has been built in to the new version is breathtaking. Witness Figure 10.15—a slide of imported images. The original photos are all rectangular and unadorned; nothing was been to any of them with outside software. All of the perspective shifts, shadows, cropping, and framing are one-click options with the new release.

Download 10-15.pptx and open with PowerPoint 2007.

In some cases, one click is all you get and in other cases, you get more control than you might ever need. Having these controls internal to the application is terrific; nonetheless, I see a long and prosperous partnership between PowerPoint and a good graphics package.

Raising Your Graphic IQ

It's an annual reality check when I ask patrons at PowerPoint Live whether they use graphics software, or for that matter if they know what a graphic is. One year, we asked for the difference between a vector graphic and a bitmap graphic and the answers were quite eye-opening:

- "Both are graphics; aren't they the same??"

- "That's too complicated—just give me something that lets me go Edit | Copy."

- "When I double-click a photo, some program opens. I'll just use that."

- "What's a graphic?"

Furthermore, we find a startlingly high number of PowerPoint users who settle for the meager tools built into versions 2003 and earlier. To them, a graphic is a star or a triangle. They take this limitation for granted and that stunts their growth as creative professionals.

Version 2007 offers dramatic breakthroughs in terms of capability but not necessarily in terms of understanding. A significant percentage of PowerPoint users are likely to continue clicking buttons to make things happen and go on not understanding the field of graphics.

This phenomenon is not limited to those in the presentation community; we see a world-wide indifference toward creative tools that were once considered de rigeur. We note two reasons for this:

- Today, most people associate computer-based graphics with digital photography, where the hardware purchase is seen as tantamount. Cameras usually come with a CD of software and whatever (often meager) programs are present on that CD make up that person's creative suite. People no longer pay attention to the difference between vector and bitmap graphics; they just want something that can work with their digital photos.

■ The default choice for bitmap graphics, Adobe Photoshop, is very expensive. Even though the cheaper Elements version is under $200 and would satisfy most users' needs, the $649 for Photoshop CS or the $1,200 for the Creative Suite is what gets their attention in the way of severe sticker shock.

This is why I have been pleased to see Corel make an effort to appeal to the presentation professional with its CorelDraw Suite. For pricing less than half of Photoshop, you can purchase a bundle that includes vector-drawing and bitmap-editing programs, both offering more power than you'd ever need.

◆

However you get there and with whatever program you choose, becoming proficient with graphic software is key to your development as a presentation designer. Suddenly, you have answers to questions that might have plagued you over the years:

I have a PDF file with text and photos that I want to use; how do I do it?

Answer: you open the PDF file in a graphics program that knows how to separate out its parts, and then you export the parts you need as separate files.

I received a logo from a client and it looks like hell. What can I do with it?

You can recreate it in a good vector graphic program, possibly using a tool that will automatically trace the logo for you.

The client's logo came to me as an EPS file and my version of Power-Point can't load it.

Open the EPS file in your graphic program and then export it in a different format. (PowerPoint 03 can read EPS files better than earlier versions, but not as well as graphic software.)

The stock photo I purchased of a race car has a terrible background, full of people working in the pits and cars strewn around. What can I do?

You can remove the race car from the scene and place it in a better scene.

The photo of the girl blowing out her birthday candles has a snot-nosed kid next to her.

Remove him, using the Clone tool of any image-editing program.

The photo is way too dark.

Adjust the exposure.

I want to take the background of my main photo and (pick one) blur it, make it black and white, vignette it, duotone it, recolor it, change its perspective, apply a stained glass to it, add rain, snow, or fog, or do about a thousand other things that I can't yet even imagine.

You get the idea...

Chapter 11

Thriving with Animation

Chapter Five concluded with the following statement:

> **When done correctly, animation can be a beautiful thing.**

Do you recall that? Do you recall reading that and then hurling epithets in my direction? Did you accuse me of hallucinating? After all, when is the last time you remember a PowerPoint animation being beautiful? There are two reasons why the answer might be never:

- Animation might be single-handedly responsible for more PowerPoint annoyance than all the other annoyances combined. Between Edward Tufte and Dilbert creator Scott Adams, PowerPoint animation is publicly flogged more often than our politicians are.

- When done correctly, animation isn't noticed at all.

Good PowerPoint animation is so seamless that you are unaware of it. It reaches its zenith when it allows audience members to become lost in the story you are telling.

I approach this chapter with the same fear and trepidation that I do our seminars on the topic at PowerPoint Live. This chapter, and the one that follows, will be the most widely-read in the book, just as our seminars on the subject invariably play to standing-room-only audiences. I know that your appetite for the subject is insatiable, and that your zeal could send you across the bounds of good taste a few times.

And when that happens, it's my fault. I'm helping you commit Death by PowerPoint. So please repeat after me, placing your left hand on a stack of Archie comics:

- I will use custom animation wisely and appropriately.

- I vow not to offend the sensibilities of my audience.

- I promise not to use an animation technique simply because I just discovered it.

- I swear never to make stuff move on screen just because I like to watch my audience members' heads bob and weave like drones.

Wisely and Appropriately

If you put 10 PowerPoint content creators in a room, you might get 11 opinions about what constitutes "wise and appropriate" animation.

Sandra Johnson's definition: "Good animation delivers useful information with storytelling techniques. Using animated 'infographics' allows the presenter to visually convey the story when static images are not sufficient."

Figure 11.1
Can you learn golf this way? No chance...

Getting started with the game

The Basics of a good golf swing

Shopping Cart

- Spine upright or beyond at followthrough
- Front shoulder high to promote balance
- Head perfectly level
- Elbow at 90 degrees to maintain club face angle at impact
- Hands at or above ear to avoid slice
- Club face wrapped around body for maximum torque.

Figure 11.2
Still not good
enough!

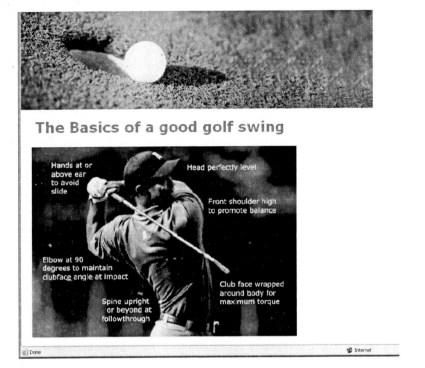

Kathy Jacobs' definition: "Good animation focuses audience members on what they need to know and doesn't keep them from understanding the content."

My definition: Good animation promotes increased understanding and appreciation of a topic. It calls attention to the topic, not the tool.

The goal of any animation should be to highlight a slide's story, being careful not to overshadow that story with inappropriate wizbangery.

Those who have attended my seminars have heard this anecdote before. It involves a friend who created a prototype web site for golf enthusiasts, of which I am one. This was to be a hybrid of news, equipment, and instruction, and Figure 11.1 showed his idea for one of the instructional pages.

Now I don't know about you, but I've been playing golf for over 30 years and to this day, a triple-bogey lurks around every grassy knoll. Golf is way too difficult to learn from the web equivalent of a slide full of bullets. His development team told him no less, and so he went instead with the page shown in Figure 11.2.

This was better, but still, you can't appreciate the mechanics of a good golf swing from a static image. A beginning golfer needs to

Figure 11.3
The dynamic of a good swing comes into focus when you see it as part of a sequence.

understand the sequence of events that make up a sound swing, and that cannot come from a single photo.

Figure 11.3 is much improved. The graphic on this page has been replaced with a Flash file (which you're seeing in mid-build), and each point appears in sequence. Now this is useful!

Surf to www.betterppt. com/11-03.htm to see this Flash animation.

In many respects, this Flash file is one of the finest examples of animation I have ever seen, even though it is entirely devoid of any of the custom animation effects that we are accustomed to using. Each point appears, two seconds after the other, that's all. Yet it helped immeasurably in telling the story of a good golf swing.

This is what we should all aspire to: the simplest use of animation that promotes increased understanding among your audience members.

You will notice that slide transition is part of this discussion about animation. We see anything responsible for sequencing elements and creating motion as part of the animation scheme, regardless of what PowerPoint calls it.

Three Steps to Better Animation

Would that every one of us use PowerPoint animation only to control the sequence and timing of events. Nobody would ever be annoyed by obnoxious animation again. That is not realistic for a number of reasons—some of them legitimate and some of them maddening—so we begin by acknowledging that a certain amount of animation is inevitable. That is Step 1 in a three-step approach.

1. Define your baseline

Every PowerPoint project has a certain rhythm to it, and the extent to which you identify that meter can help you animate it properly. I like to refer to this as a presentation's *baseline* animation.

Download 11-04.ppt to see for yourself.

Take a look at Figure 11.4, a snippet from a beginning workshop on digital photography. Across the seven content slides, the identical title is used and an effective animation scheme would have the title always displaying. You would want to animate these slides as follows:

1. On the slide master, apply a wipe or fade to the bullets.

2. Set Slide Transition to No Transition.

This way, as you advance from slide to slide, the title never moves —it is omnipresent. New content appears with a simple animation.

Baseline for this presentation: No slide transition, bullets on Wipe Right.

Figure 11.4
The best animation scheme for these slides is to leave the titles alone and apply a simple animation to the bullets.

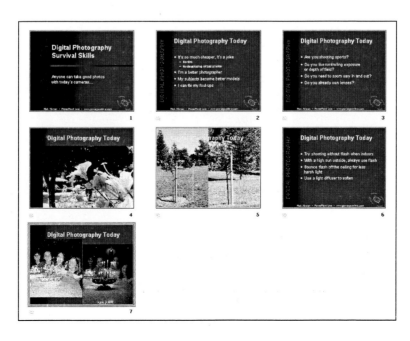

Figure 11.5
This presentation needs a baseline that wipes the slate clean often.

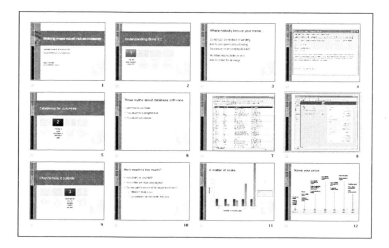

Now check out Figure 11.5, a seminar about effective email campaigns for marketing and P.R. professionals. Even from these small thumbnails, you can see that these slides are quite varied—lots of title changes, different layouts used, various types of builds employed. These slides have stark changes, either in topic or in layout. They need an eraser. The best animation scheme for this presentation is to begin with a slide transition of a slow or medium fade or a slow wipe from left to right. That's the eraser—after that, you can begin to build the new content.

With so many slides representing new topics, it is best to display the title by itself before introducing the new content. This gives the presenter a chance to frame the topic if he or she chooses. Therefore, each first item after the title should be brought in On Click.

Figure 11.6
These slides just need to be delivered to the screen in a consistent way.

Baseline for this presentation: Wipe or Fade slide transition, first bullet On Click.

Figure 11.6 shows the seminar that Echo Swinford delivered for PowerPoint Live on this very topic: animation. Each slide introduces a new topic but the content of each slide does not need to be framed or introduced—it can just be displayed on screen and then spoken to.

Download 11-06.ppt to watch this animation.

The audience needs to know that each slide represents a new topic, so the slide transition should not be subtle. And with the bullets tagging along directly behind the title, there should be unity in the animation.

Baseline for this presentation: Slide transitions wipe slowly from left to right, bullets wipe down from the top quickly.

Part Two: The Solution

A Word About Pace

Speed kills, as the adage goes. With presentations, so can the lack of speed. Choosing the proper pace for your animation, especially your baseline animation, can often mark the difference between success and failure. When you slow the pace at which your objects appear on screen, you raise the bar of expectation, whether you mean to or not. You send the message to your audience members that this element deserves extra attention. If it doesn't, then you are crying wolf.

My rule of thumb, scientifically proven by nobody, is to animate text at twice the speed at which it can be visually scanned.

On the other hand, complex ideas need to be doled out carefully, so as not to short-circuit your audience. The horizontal axis for a complicated graph should be wiped from the left slowly and you should pause before placing the data points onto it. When you slow the pace here, you assure your audience that you will give them the time they need to see both the forest as well as the trees. They can relax.

It's almost impossible to set slide transitions too slow because the speed settings that the program developers offered are quite blunt. Fast is way too fast, Medium is too fast, and Slow is usually just about right, unless you want to call attention to a transition, in which case Slow is too fast also. When I want to slow down the transition of a slide, I usually fake it with custom animation, which can be set to any speed: apply exit animations to the current objects, transition with no visible effect, and then animate the entrance of objects.

2. Determine secondary animation

This category of animation is best not used. Okay, next topic...

I'm only half-kidding. Knee-jerk animation runs rampant in this category, as "just say no" has not reached many corners of the presentation community. As Captain Picard and Commander Ryker heard on more than one occasion, resistance really does appear to be futile. People just can't resist.

I define secondary animation as motion applied to elements of a slide *after* they have made their initial entrance. Nine out of 10 times, elements don't need any motion beyond their entrance; I wish content creators would resist nine out of 10 times.

But there are many scenarios in which secondary animation is exactly what a slide needs, and Figure 11.7 shows one of the most common: the introduction of charted data.

This chart looks at the time requirements of an email campaign and the wisdom of using an outside service to assist you. There are two things that are noteworthy about this data: 1) If you use an outside service, the time required is the same, irrespective of whether you send out a handful or an ocean full of emails; and 2) the time required to send out 10,000 emails by yourself is literally off the charts—we needed to create that bar outside of the graph.

Figure 11.7
Taken in all at once, this chart is not nearly as illuminating as if you were to sequence the information. Good animation is all about sequencing.

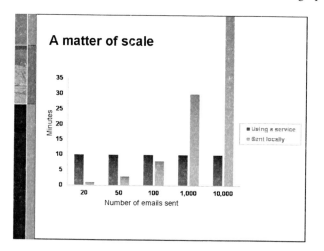

Proper animation of this chart can make all the difference in the world to your audience's appreciation of the point you are trying to make. Most content creators recognize that something should be done to charts like this, but they don't think it through—so instead, they give the entire chart some weird animation, like a box in, or diamond out, or those Venetian blind thingies.

Calling attention to the chart is not necessary; it's the only thing on the slide. What is needed here is to *direct* attention, and that requires more thought. Here is how we would go about it:

1. Select the chart and apply a Wipe animation, On Click, From Bottom, Very Fast.

2. In the Animation task pane, open Effect Options for the animation and move to the Chart Animation tab.

3. For Group Chart, choose By Element In Series and check the Animate Grid and Legend box. Click OK to close the dialog.

By Element directs the animation to stop after each point, and In Series directs the animation to display one entire series ("Using a service") entirely before showing the other series ("Sent locally"). Checking the Animate Grid box draws the frame of the chart before displaying any data at all.

4. Click the downward-pointing arrows to expand the animation scheme for the chart.

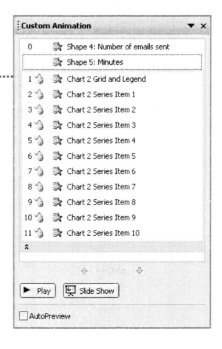

5. Decide where you want the bars of the chart to draw automatically and where you want to pause to discuss. Change the animations to After Previous when you want them to appear automatically.

6. Add Wipes to the text for each axis, using With Previous, and finally, a long, slow Wipe From Bottom for the rectangle that goes off the chart.

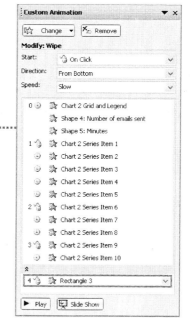

Download 11-07.ppt from the betterppt.com site and you'll see how this chart would be presented:

■ First, the axes, labels, and legend appear, while you frame the question that you are addressing: Which is a better use of time, sending quantities of email yourself or hiring an outside agency to do it for you?

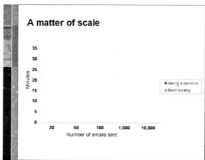

■ Then the entire first category appears at once, showing that the time spent using an outside service is a constant—10 minutes, whether the task is a few emails or thousands of emails.

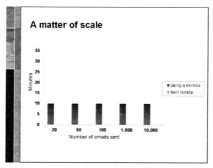

■ The first three bars of the second category display, showing the trend that favors an outside service as the volume increases.

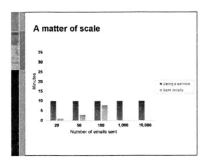

■ The fourth bar displays, confirming this trend.

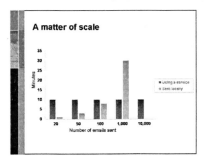

■ And your coup de grâce: the final bar moving all the way off the chart.

Several good things happen with this use of secondary animation:

Your audience really gets it: I'm a big believer in separating form and content to promote understanding. Offering up the empty chart is a great way to prepare your audience for what they are about to see.

You control the pace: Charts are almost always displayed too quickly, leaving audience members with the feeling that they're drinking from a fire hose. If you suspect that members of your audience are not clear on what it is you're about to show them, you can wait until they understand before continuing.

You become more confident: You have control of your audience in the palm of your hand (perhaps literally, if you use a wireless remote). Without being too crass about it, this position of advantage will likely manifest itself in a positive way.

You create trust: This is a great way for you to bond with them, by assuring them that you are not going to hurry them through data-heavy content. PowerPoint audiences are so often on guard in case a

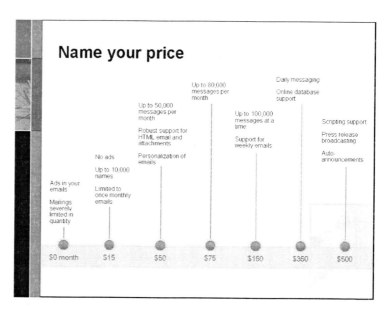

presenter does something ridiculous with animation or obnoxious with content, it's amazing that they remember anything. Give them a soft landing with a heavy slide and they'll remember it. They'll relax and be more receptive to your ideas.

With that example under your belt, think about how you might animate the infographic in Figure 11.15, a progression of prices based on level of service. If you throw it all out there, you jeopardize potential impact, understanding, and appreciation. If instead you offer your audience members the continuum of pricing, they get it right

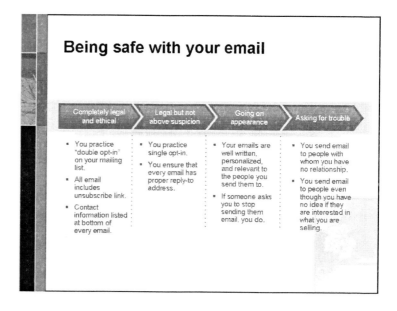

away—it's going to be a comparison of services, based on price. Now bring in each price point, one by one, speaking to it as you go.

Ditto for Figure 11.16, a continuum of email strategies from safe to unethical:

1. First wipe from left to right the four categories.

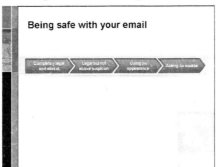

2. Without pausing, wipe the divider dots down.

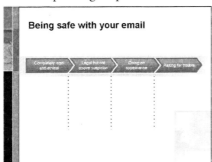

3. And then introduce each column of data on a click, speaking to it as you go at whatever pace is comfortable to you.

These steps are written as if we are speaking only to those who are to deliver this type of content. May we sit and watch 50 boomerangs for our crimes! Our advice here is equally pertinent to content creators preparing work for others to deliver. Maybe more important: content creators will have to prepare these charts and *then* explain them to the presenter.

We spoke in Chapter 7 about the potential insult associated with spoon-feeding bullets. It is an entirely different situation here. This data has to be studied, not just read. Here, spoon-feeding is a courtesy.

Sequencing information is so well-suited to the presentation medium, you can use it in situations other than the handling of data-heavy content. I got quite a laugh when I employed it in that same seminar on email strategies. In discussing the risks of not using Blind CC, and with the help of my image-editing software:

1. I first displayed a blank email message, to provide context for what I was about to show.

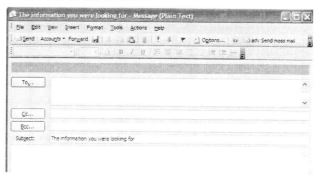

2. I then faded in the addresses, all placed in the standard location in the To field of Outlook (grayed out for privacy).

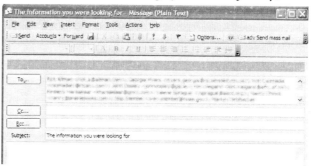

3. And then faded in the farcical letter itself, highlighting the perils of sending an email to many people at once.

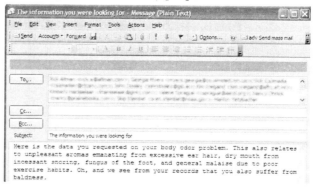

This animation technique is not rocket science, and the point of this part of the presentation was not exactly earthshaking. Most people know when to use Blind CC and when not to. But when the whole

Part Two: The Solution

room broke out in laughter, I knew that I had succeeded in using the technology to introduce a light topic in a way that set a good tone for the rest of the hour.

3. Apply supplemental animation

Technically, this type of animation would be referred to as "tertiary" (one more than secondary), but I hate that word. It's impossible to use it without sounding like a bloviating blowhard, which as we all know, is the worst kind of blowhard to be. Alas, we digress, which, given the length of this chapter, makes for a necessary mental break. Alas, I digress again. I wonder who's atop the leader board at this week's PGA tournament. Alas...

I define this category as animation that is for the benefit of the presenter, not necessarily for the benefit of the audience (although you could certainly argue that anything that makes the presenter's job easier benefits the audience).

Did PowerPoint Animation Win a Case?

According to Edward Tufte, PowerPoint brought down the space shuttle. According to our creative editor Sandra Johnson, it prevailed in litigation. And she ought to know: it was her work that might have earned her client's client millions of dollars. For a recent court case, in which a woman suffered paralysis during childbirth, a law firm hired Johnson to illustrate a complicated medical condition at the core of the dispute.

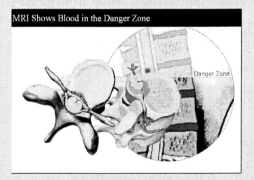

Johnson carefully sequenced the events so that the attorney could explain the situation more easily to the jury. It was effort worth making, as right after Johnson's animations were shown, opposing counsel convinced the defendant to settle. Post-trial jury comments confirmed that they would have likely found for the plaintiff after watching the presentation.

Figure 11.23
Who says you can't
show your script to
the audience?

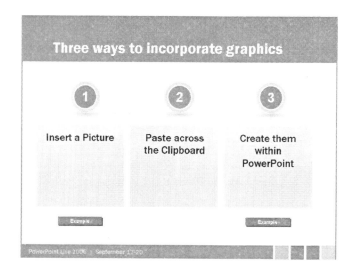

In its simplest form, I refer you back to Chapter 7 and page 46, where we discussed the little rectangle that appears after your bullets have displayed, to let you know that the build has completed.

Many presenters, present company included, are perfectly comfortable with a slide like Figure 11.23. The two small "Example" rectangles fade in to remind me about which two of these three topics have visuals that I am to show and which one doesn't.

I probably have this in my notes, but I might be across the room taking a question or just being an idiot and not looking at my notes. But I won't forget with an on-screen reminder, and I don't think there is anything unprofessional about that at all. Just the opposite—I would argue that it shows that I have my act together.

But I digress yet again. The point is that I choose exactly when these reminders appear, and I use a subtle fade so as not to be intrusive.

That was a simple example. Most of the more complicated ones fall into the category that we loosely refer to as "advanced animation," and will be discussed later:

- With Previous: Setting two objects in motion at the same time (see page 106, next chapter).

- Exit animation: Controlling how an object leaves the slide (see page 110, next chapter).

- Motion paths: Sending an object along a path (see page 113, next chapter).

- Triggers: Clicking on one object to set another object in motion (see Chapter 18).

■ Inserted Objects: Links to other presentations, other files, and other applications that can be programmed to launch as part of an animation sequence (see Chapter 18).

♦

A few things to note about the concepts we've discussed here:

Must you?

In all three categories—baseline, secondary, and supplemental—animation must pass a litmus test of necessity. Is it needed, is it helpful, will there be benefit? If you can't answer yes to these, the animation fails the litmus test and shouldn't be used. Having said that, applying a soft and quick fade to your bullets could be helpful and beneficial, but perhaps not needed. Two out of three would be good enough...

Say what?

The terms that we have coined here have been made up. If you talk to other PowerPoint users about "baseline" or "secondary" animation, they might wonder what planet you're from.

Who needs variety?

Have you noticed that we're almost 20 pages into this chapter and we have not yet recommended the use of anything other than Wipe and Fade? That's not a coincidence: you just can't go wrong with them. Without knowing anything else about your presentation, we could feel good about having you use Wipe or Fade in practically any situation. You might find an appropriate occasion to use Fly or Zoom or Dissolve, but we don't want to be the ones to suggest it!

It's just so bloody easy to make Fade look good:

1. Get four photos that even come close to relating to your topic and import them all onto one slide.

2. Layer them one atop the other, select them all, and assign a medium-speed fade, after previous, with a three-second delay.

You run that up on a slide that would otherwise have a bunch of text on it, and it will change the entire mood of the room. Guaranteed...

Download 11-25.ppt to see how easy this effect is.

♦

Animation cannot be covered in just one chapter—turn the page and we'll turn up the volume...

Chapter 12

More with Animation

We're as bad as everyone we've railed against or poked fun at: we have so much to say about animation, we can't fit it all in one chapter. Chapter 11's focus was on the appropriate times to use animation and the best ways to craft it. This chapter focuses on animation choices that are not mainstream, but potentially invaluable in creating emphasis, elegance, realism, or illumination.

Two Animations, One Moment in Time

Once the domain of the experts, the ability to set two objects in motion at the same time has now become commonplace. As with all other matters of animation, that sword cuts two ways, so first, the admonition:

> If you think that one object moving across the slide is annoying, imagine two objects running amuck at the same time.

Understanding "With Previous" opens many creative doors, and the mechanics are not at all difficult. When you set an animation to start With Previous, you command it to do its thing along with whatever animation was scheduled immediately before it. Standard After Previous animations cannot do this; they won't begin until the previous one is finished. When you use With Previous, you break that barrier. You can still stagger the sequence by adding a delay to one of them, but the fundamental difference is still in place: you can make two things happen at once when you employ With Previous.

Figure 12.1
What would happen to this fruit in real life, and can you get PowerPoint to simulate that?

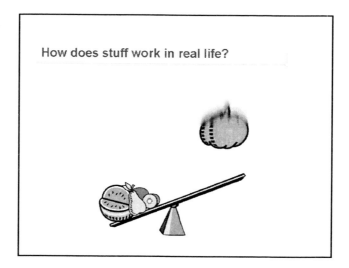

This capability finds its feet when you want to make several objects appear as one system, and I am reminded of the cute demo that we showed at the 2005 PowerPoint Live, courtesy of Julie Terberg / Terberg Design, shown in Figure 12.1.

When the pumpkin lands on its end of the teeter-totter, the fruit is going to go flying. "But how will it fly?" I asked. "If you're new to animation, it might look something like this..." after which the fruit

Figure 12.2
With Previous is the key to making this fruit fly right.

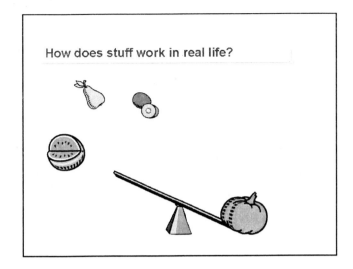

went flying...one after the other...just as After Previous would do it. People snickered.

"So then you get a clue," I continued, "and realized that they need to go flying at once...as a group." The second attempt saw the fruit fly off the slide *literally* as a group. It was hilarious—they became a big clump hurdling off screen.

By now, everyone realized where we were going with this. As each fruit would make its ceremonious exit according to its own weight, mass, shape, and personality, this was a job for With Previous, as you can sort of see in Figure 12.2.

Unlikely that you'll be sending fruit into orbit in any of your upcoming presentations, but the idea is the same: if you want to make

Figure 12.3
Animating this slide With Previous integrates all of the parts into a unified action.

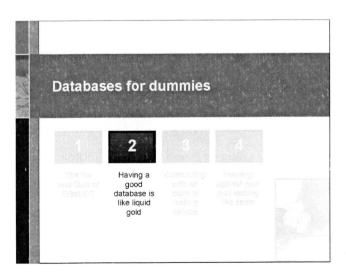

something look natural and organic, you're probably talking about using With Previous.

Back to our seminar about good email practice and the value of keeping a database of contact information: Figure 12.3 shows the segue slides I designed for new topics—title at the top, four main categories visible, all but the current one tinted back. Here is how I animated this slide:

1. I faded the slide in slowly (and remember, Slow is not very slow), revealing all four of the topics and no title.

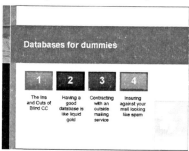

2. I set the title on a fast wipe from the left.

3. I drew rectangles over the topics *not* being discussed, two in all, and set them white.

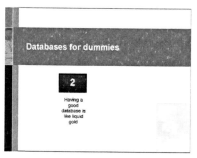

4. I applied a 20% transparency to both rectangles to make it clear that they are subordinate to the current topic.

5. Finally, I applied a fast fade to the rectangles, setting both to With Previous.

With the three elements coming in simultaneously, it creates a smooth and

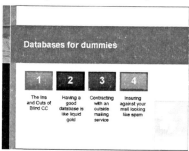

Download 12-03.ppt to see how this animation looks.

Figure 12.7
Simultaneous
animation helps
identify relationships.

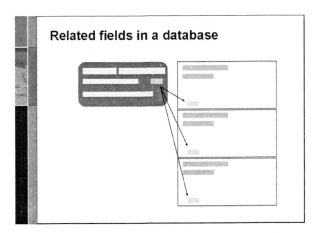

Part Two: The Solution

refined look, while at the same time acting as a roadmap for the presentation. This might not be as useful as some of the animation we saw in the previous chapter, but anytime you can show your audience an animation that is elegant and not obnoxious, it helps your credibility.

With Previous can certainly do some heavy lifting, also—witness Figure 12.7, where an intricate relationship needs to be described between elements of a complex database.

Sending several objects onto the slide at one time is key to showing which ones relate to which other ones. First, the main record of the database appears (the one on the left), and soon afterward, the frame for the related records appear, to indicate that *something* else is part of this virtual ecosystem.

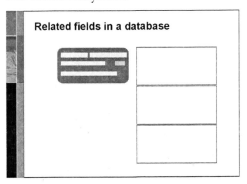

Next, the parallel fields of these related records are displayed, together. Then, the critical field for each related record that pivots around the main record displays, in a different color for emphasis.

And then some simple arrows emanate from the main record, again all using With Previous. The simultaneous quality of this animation is central to its ability to describe the dynamic relationship.

For good measure, which you can see by downloading 12-07.ppt, we faded a screen image of an actual database right atop these elements. Showing the interface atop the graphics used to describe the parts was big in helping audience members understand database theory.

Please Leave by the Exits

I haven't forgotten the first time I saw it. A medal deserves to be awarded for the most elaborate workaround by someone who never knew that an object's departure from a slide could be choreographed as readily as its entrance. Without knowing about exit animations, he went to hell and back to compensate.

It was a colleague who speaks at our CorelWorld User Conference, and he was showing various dialog boxes that appear within CorelDraw and then speaking to them. He thought it would be helpful to show the dialog boxes atop the Draw interface along with examples of what they do, and he was right. Figure 12.9 shows one in the series.

Without knowing about exit animations, when it was time to show the next example, he first created white rectangles and faded them atop the old examples. He used rectangles like erasers...except he was not really erasing the examples; he was just covering them up. With all those slide elements being obscured by solid rectangles, it was only a matter of time before anyone would go bonkers.

If all of the objects were the same size, he could have just faded new objects over old ones, but they weren't, so he couldn't. His best course of action would have been to apply exits to the old objects either right before or at the same time that new objects appear.

Figure 12.9
This interface will play backdrop to many images. How would you replace one image with another?

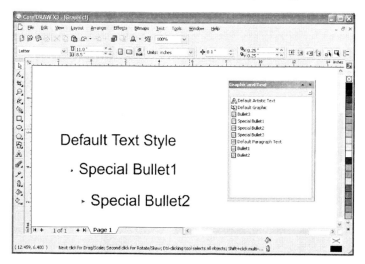

Figure 12.10
Exit animations make this illustration easy...but saturation looms.

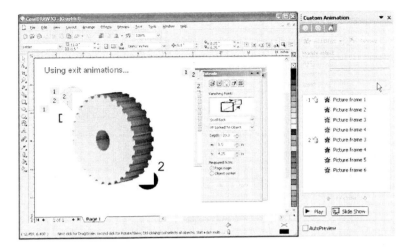

If you know how to animate, you know how to create exits—you just choose Exit instead of Entrance and do everything else the same. At the risk of oversimplification, there is nothing complicated about applying exits to elements of a slide.

Exit vs. New Slide

The biggest hurdle to using exit animations is in knowing when *not* to use them, and Figure 12.10 frames the potential dilemma that we content creators face. This is how my CorelWorld colleague could have put together his illustrations: instead of covering up each old image, he could have just created exits for them.

This is a relatively simple animation scheme, with just three sets of images that must appear and/or disappear, yet the number of overlapping objects can become frustrating. With more ambitious tasks, your patience would likely max out.

The Animation task pane exposes the other issue: selecting these objects can be a bear, due to one of our long-standing objections with the software: objects imported via the Clipboard are assigned arbitrary and sometimes obtuse names and cannot be renamed.

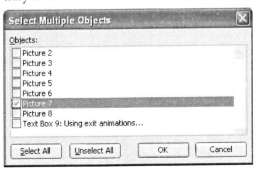

▼ Version 2007 to the rescue: While the Custom Animation engine remains largely unchanged in the brand new version, object handling has been revamped, finally allowing for slide elements to be renamed for easier identification and selection.

This is a situation where it might be easier to eschew animation entirely and just allow slide transitions to create the visual effect. Figure 12.12 shows how this would be accomplished. The program interface needs to be in the same place, so we just threw it onto the slide master. As each slide fades to the next, it creates the appearance of the elements fading out and fading in.

Figure 12.12
Slide transitions are often a better tool to use than animations.

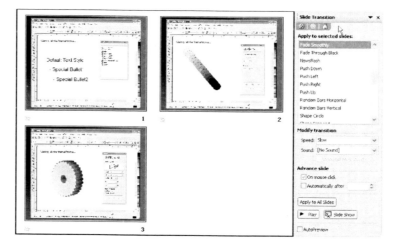

▼ Download 12-12.ppt to see both methods in action and judge for yourself.

There is no inherent advantage to using slide transitions in terms of file size or performance; it would simply be easier to build. With each transition being on a separate slide, selecting and working with the elements proves to be a friendlier experience.

Figure 12.13 offers a situation in which exit animation is the *only* way to achieve the desired effect. In this homage to the sea, the background scene slowly drifts to the right, while other evocative photos appear in sequence. This must be done on one slide, and there would be no way to cover up the images when it's time for them to leave. It's exits or bust!

There are a few important things to note about the screen image in Figure 12.13:

■ According to the Zoom tool on the toolbar, the magnification factor is 33%, meaning we are zoomed out quite a bit.

Figure 12.13
This dramatic and
sweeping montage
of photos can only
be created with exits.

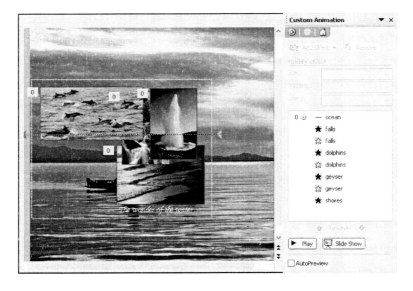

Download 12-
13.ppt to see this
mosaic of
images.

■ We have created a temporary dotted white line around the slide
to give you a sense of proportion (the background photo is
much larger than the slide).

■ The Animation task pane shows that three of the elements that
fade in then fade right back out (exit animations have lighter-
colored icons).

The Path to Motion

Many PowerPoint users overlook the Motion Path option for animation because: a) they view it as redundant to what Fly can do and
they already know how to use Fly; b) working the motion path controls can make even the most accomplished user feel like a moron;
and c) isn't it all motion, so why should I bother with something
called Motion Path when that's what all animation is?

While it's true that some of the animation choices can mimic a
motion path, and while it's definitely true that the tools can often
make you feel foolish, sometimes you just can't beat a well-executed
motion path...especially if you learn a trick or two...

Fly moves in one of four directions; arcs, ascensions, and some of the
other more ridiculous choices are similarly limited. But with a
motion path, you can move an object from any point and to any
point, without restrictions. And combining motion with other animations is exceptionally powerful.

Part Two: The Solution

Figure 12.14 is a rudimentary example of motion's value in basic tutorials. Not many people in our user community would need to be taught how to place a CD into a CD drive, but there are plenty of new PC users who would welcome this level of hand-holding. Thanks to a motion path, this CD will literally move directly atop the holder.

If you download and run this animation, you will see that the CD lands right on top of the tray...or does it? Please don't look too closely, okay? We don't really have a clue where it ends up. After about seven or eight tries of tweaking the ending arrow and then playing the slide, we achieved something that perhaps rises to the level of passable.

Our longest-standing objection with the software is its lack of coordinate points for animations that change the size or position of an element. You can't even eyeball it because while editing the slide, the element is in its starting position, not its ending position.

Throw motion in reverse

Because of this shortcoming, there is a semi-elaborate workaround that is often worth the effort. It involves a little-known ability to ask for a motion to go in the opposite direction. At the Path dropdown on the Animation task pane, choose Reverse Path Direction.

Using the Advanced Timeline

Anyone who has ever used non-linear video editing software such as Adobe Premiere or Microsoft Movie Maker would look upon the Advanced Timeline available in the Animation task pane as something akin to nursery school. Advanced? Yeah, right...

Be that as it may, sometimes we animators don't need anything more than nursery-school tools, yet a vast majority of PowerPoint users never use the Advanced Timeline, and as many as 70% do not even know that it exists.

Right-click on any of the entries in the Animation task pane and choose Show Advanced Timeline. That brings up a chronological display of the animation sequence for the current slide. Advanced or no, it often beats the stuffing out of having to right-click on every animation and work a dialog box. By sliding those orange bars around, you can:

- Set the moment when an object begins its entrance
- Control how long its entrance lasts

Figure 12.14
Better hand-holding through Motion Path.

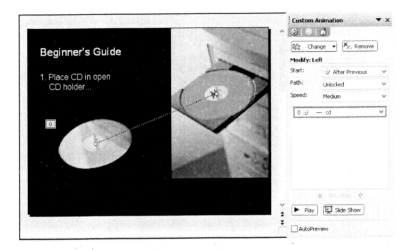

Download 12-14.ppt to see the techniques for using motion paths.

Now when you extend the line out from the element, you are defining its staring point. Now you can use your nudge keys, which, in conjunction with Shift and Ctrl, give you tremendous control over object placement. You can also use the coordinates built into the Format dialog box to get the ending location of the object just right. Meanwhile, you'll be approximating the object's starting point, but that's usually okay, as the starting point is often less important than the destination.

- How long it will reside on the slide
- When it will begin to exit

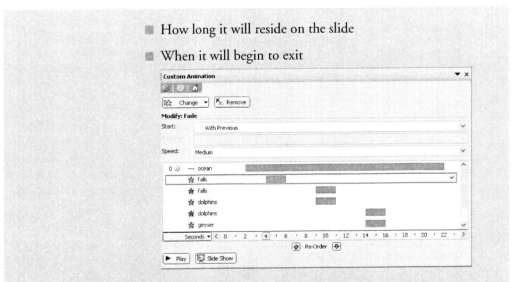

Above all, you can do this while seeing how the other elements on the slide are being handled. No element is an island, and that is especially true when a slide has elements set to With Previous or with elements whose exits are tied to the entrances of other elements.

But here's the tricky part about this strategy: when you show the slide, the object initially appears at its destination. Then when you begin the motion path, it suddenly jumps to its starting point and moves back to its destination. In the case of the CD and the computer, the CD initially appears in the tray then jumps out into the open space, then moves back to the tray.

This can be solved by one of two techniques that are more easily understood by watching than by reading about them, so we suggest you dissect them in 12-14.ppt. In general:

- You add an entrance fade to the CD and you begin its motion simultaneous to that entrance. As long as the motion begins at the same time, the CD will not appear in the tray.

- You make a copy of the computer and place it on top of the CD. As soon as the motion begins and the CD jumps to the starting point, you make the computer disappear.

This is really geeky, we know. But figuring this stuff out makes you feel on top of your game. As you get more of these geeky little victories under your belt, you'll begin to feel as if there is nothing that you can't simulate or replicate with PowerPoint animation.

Zoom!

For instance, it took a geek to figure out that you could couple the motion path with a Grow emphasis and simulate the feeling of flying over a landscape. Figure 12.16 shows a nice aerial view over a

Figure 12.16
Add a Grow to a Motion Path and you get a helicopter ride.

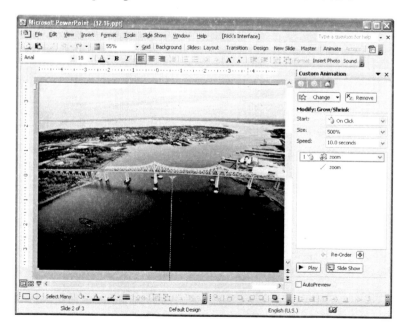

waterway, and if you study the screen image, you will find two clues for what is about to happen:

- ■ The motion line on the photo heads past the lower boundary of the photo, indicating that this photo is going to move a lot.

- ■ According to the Animation task pane, the photo will also grow in size by 500%.

In other words, as the photo is moving down (which is the same as you moving up over it), everything will be getting bigger...exactly as it would if you were flying toward the bridge in a helicopter.

▼ Download 12-16.ppt to see the effect and to see how we handle the post-zoom issue of finishing with a good-quality image.

There is one important finishing touch necessary: PowerPoint does not actually upsample the photo, so its zoom is going to be heavily pixilated. This does not become objectionable until the zoom stops, so I find it necessary to immediately replace the zoomed slide with a static slide of the same photo, sized and positioned to be identical to the final zoom.

Would that PowerPoint provide coordinates for this final location, but I've already belly-ached about that. So once again, you just have to tweak and adjust. Using a round number, like 500%, makes the sizing part easy. Nudging it to the finished location is just trial and error.

▼ Another way to zoom: Insert the picture at the size you want it to be after you zoom in on it. Add an immediate shrink animation to shrink it to the size you want it most of the time. Now, add another grow animation to put it back to full size. The end result: Smoother zooming and no pixilation.

Be Conspicuous in Your Tastefulness

As we arrive at the end of two very long and substantial chapters, I will reiterate what the most important feature is of PowerPoint animation.

Restraint.

Your audiences have seen it all. They've watched the flying bullets, the ridiculous transitions, weird things dissolving into weirder things. Just by standing in front of them and having a slide projecting onto a screen, you have already made a first impression. They have already concluded that you are probably going to be one of the countless thousands of people who will do stupid things with their slides or put them to sleep with incredibly boring content that provides no insight into the subject at hand.

Why would they think otherwise? They've seen this all before.

Every time you resist the use of a wild animation or some other gratuitous effect, you score sensibility points with your audience. You tell them "I could have done something stupid here—you know because you've seen it a thousand times—but I have conscientiously chosen not to do that."

You couldn't buy that kind of impact with all the animation in the world.

When they see that you are using animation to help tell a compelling story, they will realize how unusual the presentation is. When your slides illustrate points so cleanly and dynamically that audience members reach a higher level of understanding, you know you've got them.

Every presenter who has ever stood before an audience has some degree of ego on the line, and for most of us, there is some element of showing off that takes place.

Show off your sensibilities. Show off the fact that you understand understatement to be its own form of emphasis. Show that special form of respect for your audiences and they will remember the time they spent with you for years.

Part Three

Death, Taxes, and Public Speaking

We would like to start by telling you what this part of the book will *not* do. These four chapters will not teach you the art of public speaking. I couldn't do that if we were in the same room together—to suggest that the pages of a book could do it would be mere pulp fiction. There are some who believe that outstanding public speakers were born with their talents and all the training in the world couldn't equal that. We won't participate in that debate, because we're not interested in whether you were preordained to be a great speaker—we care only about making you better than you are right now. And on that score, there is only good news: there are real, tangible, physical behaviors that you can perform to make you a more effective presenter. And that is our focus here.

Better than Bullets

What if we told you about a visual aid that is more effective than PowerPoint and does not require the rental or purchase of an expensive projector?

The lights can be completely up while you use this particular aid and a screen is not required. You do not need extensive training to use it, and you don't have to buy a book like this. You do need to read a short chapter in a book like this, Chapter 13 to be precise, but that's all.

Best of all, you do not need to buy this visual aid. You already own it. In fact, you own two of them, and that's good, because they work best in pairs.

We refer, of course, to your hands—the best sidekick a good story-teller could possibly have. Your hands are how you direct attention, how you bring nuance to an idea, how you provide color commentary to complement your slides' play by play.

Good use of your hands involves two disparate skills: 1) acting naturally and allowing your emotions to flow freely through your body; and 2) doing nothing with them, which is much harder. We'll start with the easy part.

Communicating With Your Hands

The most important piece of advice that we can give you about your hands is this:

> **Show them!**

When you offer the palm of your hand to your audience members, you do the public equivalent of baring your soul. It is one of the most important components of the trust-building process, and trust is the first ingredient of a good relationship. This doesn't change with the size of your audience: one or one hundred, your hands might say more about you than anything else.

You might be a natural at this and not need any direction. Most aren't. Most need to make conscious efforts to work their hands into a presentation in a way that feels natural and genuine. And I can write about this until my hands fall off from writer's cramp and it won't be as effective as your seeing it in action. All of the following photos are still images taken from low-resolution video, but they capture moments in time when various speakers have become one with their hands.

One of the most polished presenters in our community is Jim Endicott, who authored the foreword for this book. No stranger to anyone who has attended PowerPoint Live, Jim describes himself as introverted, almost shy, when he is not speaking; put him in front of an audience, though, and he comes alive.

Figure 13.1 has captured one of Jim's trademark gestures, as he asks his audience "who among us wants their presenters to be perfect?" He doesn't have to verbally ask for a show of hands; by raising his own hand, he invites audience members to raise theirs. And with the "who among us," phrase, he removes potential barriers between himself and his audience. In these five seconds, and with this one gesture, he creates a connection with the room that he will be able to cultivate over the next hour.

Figure 13.1
This show of the hand is how Jim Endicott asks his audience for a show of their own hands.

Even with an audience of presentation professionals, most in the room are unaware of this complex dynamic. They just know that they're interested and engaged in what their seminar leader has to say, and our evaluations confirm this.

Jim concluded the point by sharing a personal experience and Figure 13.2 shows a body in perfect synch with the words. If he were actress Sally Field, the caption might read "You like me!" Kidding aside, arms out and palms open says to the group "I'm hiding nothing...this is the real me...I'm willing to be vulnerable." These messages resonate loudly on many levels, most of them subconscious. But set aside the

Figure 13.2
Jim invites trust with gestures that open him up.

mumbo-jumbo: You probably don't know Jim Endicott, but don't you feel as if you could place your trust in him from seeing this photo? His hands help to give you that impression.

Jim is quite deft at making gestures while holding a wireless remote. Believe me when I say that this takes practice. The first time I tried to count to one in public, while my index finger was on the slide advance button, I used my second finger. That didn't go over too well...

I leave the inspirational to experts like Jim; much of the public work that I do with PowerPoint is instructional. Therefore, I often find myself seated at a table behind a computer, actively working with a software application. While the audience accepts this physical barrier between us, I must still work hard to overcome it.

Figure 13.3 shows two such moments. No subtle gesture at my sides or even in front of my chest will be absorbed by others in the room. All of my gestures must be wide and/or high. Most of the time, my audience members are not even looking at me—they're watching the screen. And when they watch the screen, I'm not just asking them to read 24-point bullets; I'm insisting that they follow my cursor as it drives software.

Figure 13.3
Seated presenters must work their bodies and hands even more.

When I have a point to make, I have to bring their attention back to me, and I am not comfortable blanking the screen (my point might only take 10 seconds and many in the room will choose to continue to study the screen). From that seated position, I am going to have to make an emphatic gesture, requiring good posture and good computer screen clearance.

I have a simple measure for a good day leading a seminar: If my shoulders are sore and my back hurts, it means I've done well...

Figure 13.4
For her design makeover clinic, Julie Terberg was in the zone.

Julie Terberg is a brilliant designer who has chosen PowerPoint as her medium. We hired her to speak at the conference without knowing her aptitude as a presenter. We frankly didn't care—she can design such incredible slides, we figured, we'd find a way to get the knowledge out of her, even if she didn't speak English.

Julie uses personal warmth and her design instincts to tell stories about her work. Perhaps during her first year at the conference, she might have been a bit stiff (not that we remember), but by her third year, she had come into her own. Figure 13.4 shows her describing a continuum from one idea to another: "With a good color scheme, all of your decisions become easier, from simple slides [left palm] all the way to complex charts, timelines, and infographics [right hand]."

She made several references to those complex elements made easier with a well-crafted color scheme, and she was able to do so merely by holding her right hand out to the side. She had already defined that space to be "all that complicated stuff," and a wave of the hand was all that was required to refer to it later.

I suspect that she did this without awareness. When you get on a roll, you experience the best kind of intelligence, where your body knows instinctually what to do without your brain having to get involved. We athletes call it being "in the zone"—that all-too-fleeting experience where everything is working right with minimal effort.

Let's not assume—let's ask her...

[sixty minutes later]

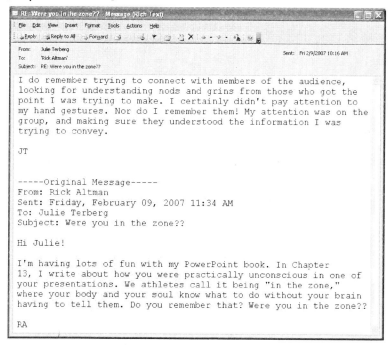

Learning How to do Nothing

With practice, you can learn to gesture more freely and effectively. If you're like me, however, you might never feel comfortable with your hands at your sides.

It's called the neutral position and it is an important place to get to, from which good full gestures with your arms are easier and carry more impact. Any audience member will readily confirm that the neutral position looks completely natural. I appreciate them telling me so, but it doesn't matter: I can't get used to it.

I keep trying, however, because I understand the value of the neutral position. In order for a gesture to have impact, it must come from a

Figure 13.6
Sometimes the hardest thing to do is just stand there.

position of rest and from a position where the hands can traverse space. Just like bold type only looks bold next to normal type, it is the contrast that makes it work. If your hands and arms are already up somewhere, gestures lose their impact.

Figure 13.6 is what my audiences insist looks normal, but to me it looks as if I have a stick up my...okay, so moving on...

I regularly mull over alternatives:

Hands behind my back: This looks relaxed, but if I hide my hands, I look shifty. Remember, showing the palm of your hand is an important gesture of trust.

Hands clasped in front of navel: I don't feel like such a dork in this position, but gestures end up getting clipped at the forearms. Before long, I look like I'm praying.

Hands together and down: This is fine for about five minutes. Then I get lazy and out comes the "flashing fig leaf"? That's when a speaker speaks so quickly, the hands can't keep up. They remain cupped in front of the private parts, except for the occasional flip of the wrists.

Hands in pocket: Too surfer dude.

One arm resting on side of lectern: This is a comfortable position, but it is not sustainable and therefore isn't neutral. After five minutes, I begin to fidget, shift my weight, cross one leg over the other, and generally act like I don't belong up there.

Holding a microphone: Now we're talking! I can walk around with a wireless hand-held all day and I have done so many times. But that's just it—it's great for being a strolling host, not as good for being an impassioned speaker. Inevitably, it gets in the way and becomes a barrier.

My best alternative, really, is to keep practicing—practicing standing in a neutral position. One of these days, I will get over on the idea that I don't look as foolish as I feel.

Just use the lectern!

This is the alternative that is most often used, and I will normally spend at least a few minutes every seminar behind one. It's not a crime to stand behind a lectern, and there are some occasions where the extra formality is appropriate. For situations where you are speaking from freshly-written notes, a lectern is tremendously convenient.

But you must understand that a large hollow box of fake wood between you and your audience members will not help you in connecting with them. You will need to work harder to compensate:

- You should pause more often, making sure to look up from your notes for several seconds at a time. Ideally, you would begin your next thought while still looking out before having to refuel and take in more notes.

- Stand as upright as you can. In fact, lean over the lectern—audiences will feel it.

- Above all, make sure your gestures are up and out in front of the lectern.

Your challenge is to find a gesture that contains energy and allows you to show emotion. Then use it—early and often! Just about everyone is going to experience some awkwardness with some aspect of physical gesturing, and you need to know that it will get easier with practice and that nobody else thinks you look foolish the way you think you do.

All I know is that I shouldn't be the only one to be made to feel like a complete moron while standing in front of a full-length mirror practicing. So if you're ever near Pleasanton California, please come visit me so we can stand in front of a mirror like morons together.

Chapter 14

Fighting Nerves

I remember the first time I came face-to-face with paralyzing nervousness, and all I was doing was sitting on a couch. It was 1978 and I was 19 years old. Six years prior, I stood up in front of 200 people and chanted in Hebrew for my Bar Mitzvah. But that was nothing compared to this scene.

It was the ninth inning of Game Two of the 1978 World Series between the Dodgers and Yankees, and L.A. rookie Bob Welch struck out Reggie Jackson to win the game. I was sweating vicariously for Welch, who looked like he was about to walk into a gas chamber. He faced Mr. October, the man with more memorable post-season homeruns than anyone, and he struck him out.

I've never seen anyone so nervous and I've never been so nervous for someone else. What I didn't consider, however, is whether Jackson was nervous. Years later, he addressed that:

> **"If I'm not nervous, then there is something wrong. If I don't feel those butterflies, it means maybe I don't care as much as I should."**

I always feel a bit better about my own public anxiety when I think of that quote, and so should you. It is neither realistic nor helpful to believe that you can quell your nerves; it would be better to learn to live with them. If the greatest World Series performer in history could do it, so can you. Here are a few strategies to try to become one with your nervous half.

The Lowdown on Laughing

This might be the oldest advice on record: start with a joke. Laughter relaxes you, it makes you feel more comfortable, and it allows you to loosen up. It is the classic icebreaker.

Well, what if you're not funny? What if your joke bombs? As Jerry Seinfeld said to George one afternoon, that's a pretty big matzo ball hanging out there.

Unless you have a joke that is guaranteed to be funny and is relevant to the topic of your presentation, the risk is too great. Besides, there is a better idea. Instead of trying to make your audience laugh...

Make yourself laugh.

I'm very serious about this (ha ha). If the audience laughs at your joke, it *might* make you feel better. If you laugh, it is virtually guaranteed to make you feel better.

> **This talk today on warehouse efficiency, it seems kind of funny that I should be the one leading it...[chuckle]...and if you ask my mother about this, she'll agree...[snicker]...because you've never seen a kid growing up with a messier room than mine. How I got to this point where I am expected to act as an authority on this subject is...[laugh]...well, that's just beyond me...**

Audience members might laugh along with you or they might not, but it doesn't matter either way. You're not trying to be comically funny, and so this isn't a joke that can bomb. It's funny to you in a reminiscent sort of way and therefore it is appropriate for you to see the humor in it.

> **You know that story about "If it's Tuesday, this must be Belgium?" I now know what they mean. This is my fourth city in four days, and yesterday I woke up and literally forgot where I was...I [laugh], I thought I was already here in Austin, about to speak to all of you. I left the hotel and immediately got lost, until I realized that I was in San Antonio. So...[laugh] to say that it's good to be here takes on a whole new meaning.**

This anecdote might not be funny to your audience but anyone can see why it might be funny to you, so again, it doesn't seem like forced humor. It almost doesn't matter what kind of story you share—*make it up if you have to.* There is nothing like a few light chuckles to change your body chemistry and increase the energy with which you start your talk.

It's easier to make yourself laugh than it is to make a roomful of strangers laugh. Easier, and better for you.

How Slow Can You Go?

It's been over 100 pages since we introduced one of our universal axioms, so here goes—Universal Axiom No. 4:

> **However quickly you think you're speaking, it will seem even quicker to your audience.**

And Universal Axiom No. 5:

> **However slowly you are speaking, you can always slow down even more.**

When you speak quickly, you do more than just make yourself nervous; you make your audience nervous. You make the whole room nervous. The projector and screen probably get nervous. The quicker you go, the more fidgety you get. You don't give yourself any time to make large gestures, so all of your gestures are small ones. Small, fast, fidgety little gestures. And out comes the dreaded fig leaf once again.

The whole thing spirals, as your fidgety gestures make you speak even quicker, which in turn makes your body try to keep up, and so your gestures become even more halting and spastic, because that's all you have time for, and the quicker you speak, the higher your voice gets, and that raises the frequency of the entire room, and through it all, *you drive your audience nuts!*

But if you slow down your speech...

...you'll slow down your entire body...

...and that will calm everyone down.

So why do we do this? It's not enough to just say we're nervous and that's why we speed up. What is making us speed up?

Much of the time, it's a fear of the unknown: we don't remember what's next. We stop thinking about what we are saying right now and begin fretting about what we are to say next. This usually happens when we are 15 feet away from our notes—swimming in the deep end, as I like to call it. *I'm out here treading water in the deep end, but I really need to get back to the shallow end* (the podium, where my notes are) *so I'd better get through this part fast!* (See page 141 for more about the deep end.)

When you know what your next idea is, it's uncanny how much easier it is to discuss your current idea. Absent of panic or dread, you can practically luxuriate in your words. And then, you can indulge in the holiest of all moments before an audience.

You can pause.

No, I mean a long pause.

Longer.

Longer still, and look at people while you pause.

This is not an awkward pause; it's a commanding pause. You have complete control of the room and everyone knows it. And how have you won the room? Why have you become so confident? Because you know where you're going. You know what you want to say next, so you can live in the moment, without panic, fear, or fig leaves.

See the discussion in Chapter 7 (page 42) about displaying all bullets at once vs. having them appear one by one. We are staunch advocates of the all-at-once practice, precisely for the reasons discussed here: it gives you context and makes it easier to focus on the current topic.

For my money, this is one of the most wonderful feelings when speaking before an audience—when I know my material so well that I can completely control the pace. I can linger on points, make extended eye contact, take questions, invite debate. Once I have established this level of control, no reasonable pause feels uncomfortable. Even if I am 30 feet into the deep end and I do completely forget what I want to say next. If I control the room, nobody will think it odd if I silently walk the 30 feet back to the lectern, spend five seconds looking at my notes, and then five more collecting my thoughts.

Anyone who has ever gone to Toastmasters or taken a course in public speaking has had to perform the exercise where you must make five seconds of eye contact with an audience member before shifting your gaze. I would argue that five seconds of silence is a better drill.

It's all made possible by your knowing what you want to say next.

Air Under the Pits

The symbiosis between the voice, the body, and the nervous system makes for a fascinating study. Unless it's *your* body we're talking about, whose byproduct of this relationship is profuse perspiration. Then it's not fascinating; it's frustrating. Each one of these parts of the system is responsible for changes in the other:

- If you are nervous, it will show in how you move your body and how you speak.

- Changes to your vocal pattern create change in body motion, which affects pulse and heart rate.

- Command over your body can create command over your speech and your nerves.

We have already discussed the syndrome whereby a nervous speaker accelerates his or her speaking pattern, which in turn causes the entire body to speed up. Whether fidgets are the cause or the byproduct of your nerves, they are not your friend, as they perpetuate the cycle and they affect your audience.

So think big.

Think about making big gestures, not little ones. Create a reason to raise both arms above your head or out to the sides. Get some air under your armpits!

Working gross motor skills is the equivalent to slowing down your vocal pattern. Your body responds more positively to a big action than to a little one. A big gesture can actually help relax you. At a minimum, it takes longer to make a big gesture than a fidget, and that alone creates a better pace for you.

I've found that raising both arms, palms up, can be interpreted many ways and audience members are generally willing to view the gesture in context.

CONTEXT: Question from an audience member about a situation that troubles her.

ME: That frustrates me too [gesture]. It's like whatever you do, it comes back to bite you. Try doing this...

CONTEXT: We solved a problem or addressed a difficult issue.

ME: [gesture] Thank the heavens, we figured this out.

CONTEXT: I ask a question and an audience member answers it correctly.

ME: [gesture] (Nothing needs to be said—the gesture serves as a "Eureka!")

Now if you feel like an idiot doing this, don't do it. The gesture has to be a part of you, but it's worth the effort to find one you are comfortable with. One colleague likes to cup his hand to the side of his head and then move it away, as if he has just had an epiphany and all this amazing stuff is flowing out of his brain. He uses that to great effect in many scenarios.

I know a woman who likes to hold one finger up, but she really goes for it, raising it well above her head. She uses it to mean "Listen up," "wait a minute," and "here's the beef."

Another uses her hands very effectively to create relationships in time, distance, or some other set of variables, just as we saw Julie Terberg do in the previous chapter. "Over here, you have the question of cost," she might say with her left palm outstretched all the way out to one side, "and over here is the issue of resources," as she stretches out her right hand. Having created those two spaces, now anytime during that conversation, she can stretch out her left palm and the audience knows she is talking about the cost factors. She has created a terrific cerebral connection with her audience...and she gets to air out her pits.

Find your own big gestures and use them to engage your audience, to improve your pace and vocal pattern, and to help quiet your nerves.

♦

As I look back on this chapter, I have to laugh. It seems as if we are advising you to become a phony:

- Fabricate a story to laugh about

- Conjure up situations in which you can make long pauses

- Make up a gesture and fake your way into using it.

But hey, let's face it, speaking in public might always feel like an artificial situation to you, so it makes sense that a few artificial devices can help you with it. Anything that helps get you to a place where you can speak naturally and share ideas freely is a good thing. So fabricate and conjure to your heart's content.

Chapter 15

Working the Room

In social or political situations, the phrase "working the room" takes on a wholly different meaning than the one we have in store for you here.

A good host for a party works the room by meeting everyone, introducing people who don't know each other, and ensuring that no glasses go empty.

If you are running for office, you work the room to gather campaign contributions and win votes.

Our definition is not nearly so captivating. It examines the physical confines of your speaking space and offers strategies for good performance. In preparing my thoughts for this chapter, I'm reminded of a golf cliché that we duffers find maddening:

The course never has a bad day.

In golf, your only real opponent is the golf course itself, and the course will never chunk a drive or skull an approach shot. It's the same with your seminar room: whatever challenges the room creates for you become your burden to solve.

To solve this for you, we thought of creating diagrams of every seminar ballroom in the United States, along with instructions on how to set them up, but our team of elves was busy in December. Instead, we'll just tell you this: unless you get to set the room up yourself, there will always be something wrong with it. Your flexibility is the most important asset you can have.

Home Base

This concept of home is one that most presenters and most members of an audience understand but rarely think about. We want you to think about it. Home not only creates comfort for you, it creates comfort for your audience. Home is where you would go to:

- Check your notes if you have them. And when in doubt, have them. Unless you have been delivering the same speech for years, don't rely on your memory and don't rely on your bullets to guide you through a presentation.

- Take questions.

- Drink.

- Pause.

The best home base is one that is raised up from table level and off to one side, preferably the left side when facing the screen. If you enter a room to find a single head table in the middle of the room, ask if you can move it and ask for a table-top lectern or a rolling podium. In either case, place them on the outside of the table.

▼ This advice assumes a standard setup with a projector displaying to a screen placed in the middle of the room. If the room is set with rear-screen projection, the middle of the room becomes available to you, however we still recommend you create home base to the left of the screen.

If your only possibility for home base is a standard table, your notes will be further away from you than normal and the risk is higher of them creating psychological distance between you and your audience. At a lectern, you only need to look down a short distance to see your notes—you can probably do it just by moving your eyes. But if your notes are on a table, the geometry worsens. The angle and the distance from your head to your notes both increase. At a minimum, you'll wish you had printed them in a larger typesize. Here are some tips:

- Spread your notes across the table so every page is visible. Don't leave them in one stack.

- Make prominent marks at your transition points. You need to be able to see where they are at a glance.

- Take questions often, and every time you call for questions, do it from home base and use that as an opportunity to check your notes.

- Be mobile. It's a long way down to your notes from a standing position, and the more stationary you are, the more you call attention to that distance. But if you can sneak a peak while you are walking up to the table, walking away from it, or even just turning to one side of the room or the other, it is less conspicuous. This is not easy to do—it's like walking, talking, chewing gum, patting your head, and rubbing your tummy all at the same time. If that becomes too much to think about, forget it.

The head table dilemma is why many colleagues of mine travel with folding lecterns that can be placed on a table. Getting your home base raised up a bit is always more comfortable.

The downside of this is if you become a prisoner to it. As discussed in Chapter 13, a lectern or podium can become a barrier, and we are not suggesting that you spend 60 minutes behind it. Home base is not where you live; it's where you retreat to at various intervals.

Going Out into the Deep End

I know that we're mixing our analogies something awful in this chapter, but here comes another one: home base is like the shallow end of the pool, where it's safe and comfortable. Your notes are nearby and you can rest your hands on the lectern.

And if home base is the shallow end, venturing forth from it is like treading water in the deep end of the pool. We wrote about this last chapter: It can be a bit scary out there, and that's why it's a good idea to plan your trips.

Going into the deep end is important—your audience needs to see you front and center, away from your notes, away from lecterns and tables, without barriers. Just you, them, and your hands. But if you get stuck out there, you could drown. This usually happens when you run out of things to say and forget what you want to say next. It's okay if you don't remember every topic to discuss—that's what your notes are for. But if it happens when you're in the deep end—that's bad.

Part Three: Public Speaking

So look over your notes and find a time when one topic moves so naturally into another topic that you will never forget. That's the time to head to the deep end. We discussed this in the last chapter (page 134): when you know your next transition, that's the time to lose yourself in the presentation, without worry or fear of losing your place.

Get out there in front of your audience, make lots of eye contact, pause often, vary the pace of your delivery, take questions, ask if anyone needs you to repeat the last point, or don't ask, just do it, to emphasize its importance. And then pause some more.

You know that you can stay out in the deep end all the way through to the middle of the next topic, before you have to swim back to shallower waters and consult your notes.

These are the times when you could be at the top of your game—when you are in command of your content and the pace with which you deliver it. Look for places in your notes where you know your

Figure 15.1
Good notes should tell you not only what to do but when to do it.

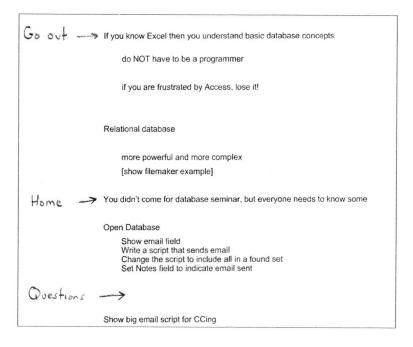

content and your transitions well and get out there right in front of your audience. In Figure 15.1, I have identified in my notes when I intend to swim in the deep end and when I need to come home.

Why return home?

The simplest reason to return to your home base is if you know there is a passage of your presentation that you will not be able to remember. We're not talking about remembering a passage word-for-word, which you should never try to do. We're referring to a passage that you forget to even bring up. The one where, 10 minutes later, you realize that you skipped entirely. Your best defense against forgetting these passages is to not even try to remember them—just schedule regular trips back home where your notes will remind you.

Other times to return home:

■ If you intend to quote somebody or read a short passage from another work. Don't try to do this by heart—it's fake. If you are reading a quote or passage that somebody else wrote, read it!

Johnny, It's Time to Come Home...

Your notes can tell you when it's time to head to the deep end, but they won't be as helpful in bringing you back. In Chapter 7, we discussed a strategy that you can implement to ensure you know when the last bullet on a slide has displayed (on page 46, involving an inconspicuous rectangle or other object that automatically appears after the last bullet). You can use this same strategy to notify you when you should return home.

1. Identify the parts of your presentation that you know really well and the places where you would be more comfortable working from your notes.

2. Create a thin rectangle, fill it with a color close to your background, and place it on the edge of the slide or in some other place where it can be inconspicuous.

3. Animate it to Appear, After Previous.

4. In the Animation task pane, move it up or down until it is in the desired place in the sequence of animated events. If necessary, move it in between a set of bullets.

1	Rectangle 3: Succeeding in business today
2	Multitasking is key
3	The new definition of team player
	Rectangle 5
4	Gadget central: how wired are you?
5	New marketing avenues are changing the rules

When the rectangle appears, it means it is time to return home to consult your notes.

- If you want to relate an anecdote that has a fair level of detail. Trying to remember those details could sprain your brain.

- When it's time to change the pace of the presentation. Being in the deep end can be tiring for you; it can also be taxing on audience members. They too experience a heightened sense of awareness by your swimming in the deep end. Returning home provides everyone an opportunity to relax.

Where does your notebook computer belong?

Many presenters place their notebook at home base and simply use the internal display as their notes. Some configure PowerPoint to show the notes page on the internal display.

These strategies are fine...as long as you can take your eyes off the damn thing. Remember Universal Axiom No. 3:

> When stuff moves on screen, your audience has no choice but to watch it.

With your notebook on the lectern right in front of you, you become a member of the audience in this regard: every time there is an animation, your eyes are going to go to it. This argues for your removing all unnecessary animation (I can hear John Lennon singing it now..."You may say I'm a dreamer...") and/or your spending more time in the deep end...both good things.

Many presenters prefer to place their notebooks closer to their audiences. I know several who reserve the middle seat in the front row, right next to the projector, for their notebooks. This way, they can easily keep tabs on what their audience members are seeing behind them without having to change the angle of their gaze much at all.

Cuts down on having to buy VGA extender cables, too...

When not to go into the deep end

The smaller the room, the less opportunity there is to swim in the deep end. In the smallest of rooms, going out into the deep end will feel stupid. In a conference room, for instance, where a dozen or so people are watching you from around a table, you can make eye contact with everyone from your lectern and your gestures will be received by all with no problem.

In a room of that size, the geometry changes. I predict you would feel awkward, maybe even foolish, if you went parading around the table, and even a journey of 10 feet or so would require that the others in the room pivot in their seats in order to watch you.

In this situation, moving off to one side of the lectern so everyone can see all of you is entirely sufficient.

Rule of thumb: if your journey into the deep end requires that audience members turn their chairs or their bodies in order to see you, you're in too deep.

Becoming One with Your Bullets

I'm already on record, emphatically, about my belief that bullets are better displayed all at once than one by one (Chapter 7, page 42). The advice offered in this chapter reinforces that opinion: there is nothing more comforting when you're in the deep end than knowing that all of the points you intend to make about a particular topic are displayed on screen.

There are other strategies that you can adopt to help you work more seamlessly with a set of points that you have displayed for your audience, and they all come down to physical positioning.

We have alluded several times in this chapter to how it's better for you to be to the left of the screen (when facing it) than to its right. Granted, working the room effectively implies connecting with all of your audience members, and you do that best when you visit every corner of the stage (keeping in mind our qualification above, "When not to go into the deep end"). However, when you are speaking directly to a series of bulleted points, your position in the room can go a long way toward helping the audience absorb them.

Figure 15.3 is a pretty bad photo of me speaking to a slide, but it's a good visual of this issue. As I discuss each of these points, I am

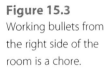

Figure 15.3
Working bullets from the right side of the room is a chore.

Part Three: Public Speaking

Figure 15.4
From the left side, you become the first component of each bullet, exactly as it should be.

referring my audience members to the screen, either implicitly, or as is the case here, explicitly.

This is a 10-foot screen that I am working with, so each bullet point spans a distance of about seven feet. If I want them to look at me, and I also want them to read the bullets, I'm asking them to play visual ping-pong: look at me over on the right, and then head all the way over to the left side of the screen to read the bullet.

It is better for you to work a bullet slide from the left side, as I am doing in Figure 15.4. Now your audience members can flow more smoothly from me straight through the bullets. For cultures that read from left to right, it is better for you to position yourself this way.

This might never register on a conscious level, but in an environment where you are trying to create an emotional connection as well as an intellectual one, it is simply one more opportunity to make your audience feel more comfortable during the time they spend with you.

The Presenter's Triangle

This suggests an entire strategy for positioning that is worth your consideration, even if you ultimately reject it for being too confining, too restrictive, too anal, too whatever. It goes something like this:

1. On the left side of the room, draw a line from the left-most audience member to the left edge of the screen.

2. That line helps defines a triangle, in which you can comfortably circulate, without fear of being in anyone's view of the screen.

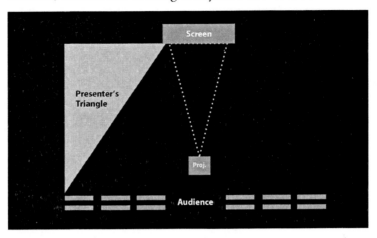

3. When you want to speak to points on the screen, you would move to the back of the triangle, near the screen.

4. When you want to make a strong point, you would move to the front of the triangle.

5. When you want to just talk, you would find a point in the middle of the triangle, and that is where your lectern could go to define home base for you.

Indeed, this is quite anal, and following it to the letter could reduce you to a robotic drone, to say nothing of ignoring those on the right side of the room. Many good presenters define triangles on both sides of the screen:

■ For bullets, they use the back of the left triangle.

■ For less specific imagery, like photos or charts, they know they could use the right triangle.

■ They head out to the tips of either triangle for emphasis.

■ And they define mid-points on both sides for neutral speaking.

The Magical B Key

We've spent a fair amount of toner in this chapter discussing how you can create the best possible relationship with your projected content. We would be remiss if we didn't mention the best way of all to do this.

Turn off the projector

Axiom No. 3 is more powerful than you think. Stuff doesn't have to move on screen to compel an audience to look at it—it just has to project. If it's there, people are going to look at it. And if it's been there for awhile, and you're not speaking to it any longer, it's now just digital flotsam.

There is no better way to refocus attention than to blank the screen. And you can do that with one click:

- Press B to turn the screen black.

- Press W to turn the screen white.

- Press the Blank button on your wireless remote.

If available, that third choice is the best, but even if you have to retreat home or head to wherever your notebook is to do it, it's worth doing when a slide has gone stale and/or you want all eyes on you.

In all three cases, the key or button is a toggle: press it again to redisplay the screen.

When you blank the display, the expectation is that the screen sinks into the background of the room. In this decade, with projectors becoming so bright, it is common for us to present in rooms with the lights all the way up. In this case, I wonder what's better: white or black? I don't know the answer to this, but I'm looking forward to somebody conducting a study.

I do know this, however: the screen should only go blank when you want it to, so please turn off your screen saver...

Mythbusting

Let's end this chapter by challenging a few of the conventional points often made about presenting to an audience.

Myth No. 1: Don't cross in front of the screen

If you never cross in front of the screen, how do you get to the other side of the room? I've seen presenters go to inordinate lengths to avoid committing this unpardonable sin, including walking down the aisle to walk around the projector and (true story) walking behind the screen.

Please.

If you need to move to the other side of the room, please just walk in front of the screen! Don't look into the projector and don't stop or dilly-dally. If you can keep your train of thought and continue speaking, it will seem perfectly natural. Trying somehow to avoid the screen will appear contrived, unnatural, and ultimately far worse than whatever perceived transgression is associated with casting a shadow on the screen.

Myth No. 2: Never turn your back to your audience

I once saw somebody trip over a chair trying to walk backwards, so obsessed was he with heeding this advice. Once again, common sense must be allowed to prevail, otherwise you're going to do yourself far more harm than this supposedly bad thing could possibly do to you.

I turn my back to the audience every time I venture out into the audience. I walk out there and then I walk back. If I walk back while continuing to speak, nobody even notices it.

Myth No. 3: Don't look at the screen

This is a younger cousin to the never-turn-your-back myth, and it's pure crap. How come everyone else gets to look at the screen and you don't? They're your slides, you know!

Looking at the screen is more than perfectly appropriate; it's an essential device to direct attention. If you look at the screen, it is virtually guaranteed that every member of your audience will, too. You don't need to turn away from the audience to do this (not that there's anything wrong with that; see previous myth)—you just need to shift your angle and your gaze in that direction.

And really, what's the alternative? If you look at your notebook computer screen instead, it's a disconnect on several levels. Now you're looking down at something that they don't get to see.

Everyone is looking at the screen; it is completely natural for you to do so, too.

Myth No. 4: Laser pointers are rude

Now this one has some truth to it. Most people who use laser pointers haven't practiced enough, so the little dot jumps all over the place and drives people nuts. The worst is when a presenter is done pointing at something but forgets that he or she still has the laser on, sending the little dot careening all over the screen.

You really don't need a laser pointer to point at the second bullet of a four-bullet slide. If you want to talk about the second bullet, refer to it by name—the "second bullet" or "second idea". A laser pointer becomes effective when you have to call attention to an element on screen that is not so easily identified. The part of a photograph where the sun meets the horizon...the part of a clamp that failed on a fork-lift...the fifth icon from the left on the second toolbar down...these are all good opportunities to use a laser pointer.

To use a laser pointer correctly, anchor your arm to your side, don't let it float in open space. Once it is anchored, then activate the laser. Try to hover it for about two seconds, then turn it off.

Myth No. 5: Silence is bad

_____.

Chapter 16

Thoughts From The Experts

Here I sit, with the notebook on my lap, my 11-year-old daughter up past her bedtime, the dog sneezing on my feet, and my wife asleep in front of a book. Shouldn't I be writing a novel or something??

The closest I may get to novel-writing is to suggest that this chapter might be a work of fiction. Now, I have critics who claim that everything I write is fiction, so this doesn't faze me too much. But in truth, as I prepare the final chapter of this part of the book, I'm honestly not sure if it will contradict the previous three or complement them. When I'm done with it, I'm not sure if I'll be sure then, either. I'm not sure of anything. Are you sure you want to read it...?

As I look over the last three chapters, I am reminded of an episode of I Love Lucy from 1954. Ricky and Fred take up golf and turn Lucy and Ethyl into golf widows. They decide to take up the game, too, and during a lesson, Lucy hears 15 individual pointers (knees bent, elbow straight, wrist firm, back slightly tilted...that kind of stuff) and attempts to incorporate all of them at the same time. The resultant swing that she perpetrates is physical comedy at its finest.

I wonder what would happen if you took all of the advice over the last three chapters and tried to incorporate them at once. Would you end up like Lucy? Maybe I have done nothing more than ensure paralysis by analysis. If I were you, I would get my money back for this shoddy excuse for journalism right now.

If I have turned you into knots trying to keep up with all of the points made in Part Three, read this chapter instead. It takes a big step back and offers quotes from noted presenters and commentators on the presentation community. In the process, you just might find some common principles essential to being a good presenter.

Know Your Audience

When asked, dozens of public speakers waste not a moment to turn the equation 180 degrees. It has less to do with you, they say, and more to do with your audience. Stand on the left...stand on the right...turn here, don't turn there—none of that matters, according to this point of view, if you don't have a firm grasp of what your audience is looking for, why they chose to show up, and with what they hope to walk away.

Emma Crosby
Anchor for Sky News

"You have got to imagine that you are talking to just one person who is in their living room or in their office. You have to think about them constantly, inform them as much as you can, and more importantly ask the questions that they want the answers to."

Anthony Frangi
Author, Successful Business Presentations

"What makes a good presenter? Someone who can stand up and gain the respect of an audience, no matter what size.

"Good presenters know their subject matter inside out and it shows. When a person is passionate about the topic, their eyes light up, body language is positive and their voice excitable.

"Becoming a good speaker means you must learn to work or connect with your audience. A presentation is for the benefit of an audience. Effective communication skills are essential for anyone in business. Standing up to make a presentation is not just about opening your mouth."

Be Yourself

Experienced presenters learn something that inexperienced presenters do not, simply because it takes years upon years to learn this: audiences do not want perfect presenters. They want presenters who are more or less like them. They want to be able to relate to them, and nobody can relate to perfection.

Jim Endicott
Presentations Coach
President of Distinction Communication

"Several years ago I found myself watching a television show called the Actor's Guild. Every week they bring in Hollywood stars who are interviewed about their careers and asked questions from an audience of young acting students. One particular week they had Keifer Sutherland from Fox's hit series 24 on the show. One of the acting students asked him what piece of advice has most shaped his very successful career. Without hesitation he said it was something that his dad, Donald Sutherland, told him when he first got into acting. He said, 'Keifer, never let them catch you acting.'

"With just slight adaptation of the concept, there's an important principle here for today's business communicators

Never let them catch you presenting.

"There's something that fundamentally changes in the nature of human beings when they go into 'presentation mode.' Some rise above the moment and maintain a critical authenticity while most get caught up in their remote pointing devices, PowerPoint and electronic projectors. Their warm smiles get replaced with emotionless faces. Meaningful eye contact is exchanged for impersonal scanning of crowds and screen watching. Methodical delivery of content is substituted for passionate and conversational speech.

"Here's the point: The art of presenting is first and foremost a relational skill. The very best presenters are those who have resisted the idea that being a good presenter has anything to do with presenting in the first place."

Geetesh Bajaj
Microsoft PowerPoint MVP,
Editor, indezine.com

"Sincerity starts it all since that ensures that the presenter believes in every word contained in the presentation, slides, notes, concept, etc. Then that sincerity brings forth some amount of confidence, but this

Guy Kawasaki

Chief Evangelist for Apple in the 1980s and now a venture capitalist

The 10-20-30 rule

I hear pitches from entrepreneurs every day. Sixty slides in their pitch: They only need 1% of the market, patent pending, unique this, proven that. Every one of them says how terrific they are.

Because I have to listen to this crap, I came up with the 10-20-30 rule.

10 slides or less, not 60.

I don't care if you have a curve-jumping, paradigm shifting, google-adword-optimized, SQL-based way to sell dog food on line.

20 minutes or less

You might have an hour window for the meeting, but if you have a Windows laptop, it might take you 40 minutes to connect it to the projector. Everything you have to say to me you should be able to say in 20 minutes or less.

30 point type

Never use a type size less than 30 point. That way, you'll put a lot less text on your slides, and that will force you to actually know your presentation, to just put the core of the text on your slide.

If you need 10pt, it's because you don't know your material so you're going to have to read it from the slide. If you start reading your material because you don't know it, your audience will figure out that you are a bozo. They're going to say to themselves, "This bozo is reading his slides. I can read faster than this bozo can speak. I will just read ahead."

If you don't buy that 30 points is the right size, I'll give you an algorithm. Find out who the oldest person in the audience is, divide his or her age by two. That's your optimal font size.

amount of confidence should not venture into the area of over-confidence."

Anthony Frangi

"Becoming a good presenter is about being yourself. Don't ever try to mimic another speaker. Letting your personality take over allows the audience to see the real you. In return, they will respect any comments you might make and adopt any advice given.

"A good speaker must be able to appeal to an audience on various levels—political, emotional, etc."

Being Prepared

The Boy Scouts' credo certainly has its place in the presentation community, and it's most conspicuous in its absence: ill-prepared presenters tend to rely on their slides and this turns them into drones. But well-prepared presenters rise well above their slides by the simple fact that they don't need them.

Tom Bunzel
Author, Solving the PowerPoint Predicament

"The major criterion for a good presenter is someone who really knows his sh*t—or in kinder language, is thoroughly familiar with his or her subject matter and knows how to deliver it effectively.

"This means that the audience members are getting their money's worth, whether they paid or not, in terms of receiving value for their time spent. Even in a sales presentation, a presenter who is there to provide real value is more likely to succeed than one who is there just to sell. And again, the basis for success will be knowledge of the issues facing the prospect and the ability to solve those problems."

Julie Terberg
Microsoft MVP
Presentation Designer

"A good presenter never reads from the screen and does not rely on bullet point after bullet point. The words that do appear in the presentation are minimal, perhaps key phrases or topics. A good presenter ensures that all projected text is legible to everyone in the audience. A good presenter respects the audience and tests the presentation—in the actual meeting room with all of the equipment—prior to the event."

Part Three: Public Speaking

Geetesh Bajaj

"Since the presenter is blessed with the right amount of confidence, he or she is bound to be a little nervous. This helps because then the presenter does not leave anything to chance and that butterflies-in-the-stomach feeling makes him or her walk that extra mile to keep the audience happy, convinced, and contended."

TJ Walker

President, Media Training Worldwide

Perfection: The Speaker's Enemy

It has been said that the enemy of the great is the good, but when it comes to public speaking, the enemy of great speaking is that quest to be great at everything. I work with business people, politicians and celebrities at every level of speaking skill, and the one problem that cuts through all classes of communication is the desire for some form of perfection in speaking.

Guess what—perfect speaking doesn't exist. There is no such thing as a perfect speech or a perfect speaker. Something could always be better.

I have found the single best way to improve speaking skills is to stand up and give a speech or interview while being videotaped. Then look at the tape and focus on what you like and don't like about your presentation. The problem for some of my clients is that they only see what they don't like. If they do 99 things well and botch one word, the only thing they do is criticize themselves and beat themselves up over that one word. They needlessly compare themselves to some image of perfection that doesn't exist even in their own imagination.

I believe in having high goals for yourself and doing everything you can to reach them. But if you obsess over every single negative to the exclusion of your strengths, assets and accomplishments, you end up paralyzed and depressed.

So my challenge to speakers who overindulge in self-criticism is this: watch a video of yourself and write down one thing you like about your presentation for everything you didn't like. That means if you can't find anything you like, you don't get to criticize the things you don't like.

Until the cycle of negativity is broken, it's nearly impossible for any speaker to improve.

Storytelling

It's difficult to articulate the difference between a presentation and a story, but when you hear a good storyteller, you just know. A good storyteller touches all your senses and triggers your imagination. When you supply your own imagination, you add to the story and make the presenter that much more effective.

Julie Terberg

"A good presenter pulls you in, makes you want to stand up and say 'Aha! I understand.' and 'Yes, I agree!' A good presenter tells a great story, making connections from personal experience. A good presenter is well-rehearsed, rarely referring to notes or script. A good presenter makes a speech seem effortless and conversational. A good presenter is compelling, thought-provoking, and articulate.

"A good presenter uses many memorable visuals to help you grasp ideas and concepts. Later on, those images are easy to recall as you replay the presentation highlights in your mind.

"A good presenter leaves a lasting impression."

And Finally...

"All the great speakers were bad speakers at first"

Ralph Waldo Emerson

"If you have an important point to make, don't try to be subtle or clever. Use a pile driver. Hit the point once. Then come back and hit it again. Then hit it the third time—a tremendous whack."

Winston Churchill

Part Three: Public Speaking

Make sure you have finished speaking before your audience has finished listening."

Dorothy Sarnoff, Broadway singer and author

They may forget what you said, but they will never forget how you made them feel.

Carl W. Buechner
Author and Presbyterian Minister

"Today's public figures can no longer write their own speeches or books, and there is some evidence that they can't read them either."

Gore Vidal, 1952

"According to most studies, people's number one fear is public speaking. Number two is death. This means to the average person, if you go to a funeral, you're better off in the casket than doing the eulogy."

Jerry Seinfeld

"Is sloppiness in speech caused by ignorance or apathy? I don't know and I don't care."

William Safire

Part Four

Working Smarter, Presenting Better

"I'd like to cover a few advanced topics, too," I wrote to one of several interested publishers of this book. "If there's time," came the response, "and if the page count allows it."

Reason No. 34B to publish this book myself: There is never enough time and the page count never allows it. Yet as we enter the home stretch, we suspect that a great many of our readers will see this set of five chapters as the most useful of all.

If you've made it this far, you deserve to sink your teeth into some truly advanced material, which these next five chapters seek to offer. Then we'll degenerate into an anarchy of tips and tricks in our final chapter, Junk and Miscellany, without which few books bearing my name are ever published.

Chapter 17

Building a Better Interface

This chapter will not teach you about any new special effects or nifty animation techniques, and it won't show you how to create a cool drop shadow or a transparency mask. In fact, this chapter does not contain any tips and tricks at all, at least in the conventional sense. We'll even go so far as to suggest that if you are satisfied with the way PowerPoint displays itself to you and with the overall design of the interface, you can skip this chapter altogether.

But if you have longed for better access to PowerPoint's commands and tools, you'll want to read every word of this chapter. Microsoft offers a robust (and largely hidden) capacity to customize the interface, and it takes center stage here.

This chapter includes step-by-step instructions, and we start with the basics. But the ramp is short and steep, because we presume that most of you who want to customize the interface are already familiar with it in the first place.

Tool Terminology 101

This chapter will be easier to digest if you start by learning a few terms and definitions.

Microsoft's definition of a *tool* within Windows is quite specific. At the top of the interface lives the *Menu*, and right below it is the *Standard toolbar*—although you'll discover in this chapter that it's not so standard after all. Below the Standard toolbar (or to its right if you ask for it to be there instead) lives the *Formatting toolbar*, and at the bottom of the screen resides the *Drawing toolbar*.

If you right-click an object, the *Context menu* appears at your cursor position. Unlike the other toolbars, this set of commands changes to suit the occasion: Right-click a rectangle and you'll see commands for arranging and ordering; right-click a subhead and you'll see a Font choice; right-click a misspelled word and you'll see a list of corrections.

If you've been working with the program for a few years, you have probably taken for granted where certain commands reside and the path you take to get there. But in this chapter, we will take nothing for granted and we will hold sacred none of the established defaults and conditions that are thought to be standard.

Required Options

If you consider yourself a proficient user, there is a set of Options that should not be thought of as optional. Let's start with the factory settings that are in place when you first start the program. Figure 17.1 shows how PowerPoint first greets the user of a freshly-installed copy of version 2003.

In this screen image, we have just pulled down the Insert menu, and so all of the commands relevant to inserting, adding, importing, etc. are visible. I'm sorry, did I say "all"? I meant to say "most." Actually, make that "some." Okay...a few.

What was going on in Redmond that day when they decided to create menus that do not show all of the choices available to the user? What a great way to learn an application: create menus that intentionally leave off 75% of the items that belong there. Yes, I know about the stupid chevron thing that points downward and shows the entire menu when you click it. That's just what I need in my life—a second click just to open a lousy menu.

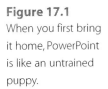

Figure 17.1
When you first bring it home, PowerPoint is like an untrained puppy.

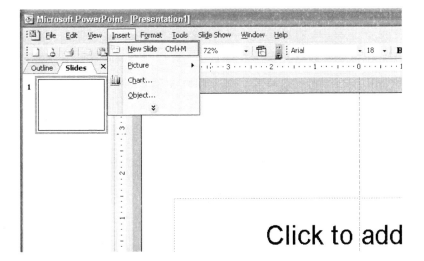

In my seminars and workshops on this topic, this is typically the point when an audience member shouts out "Tell us how you really feel."

This was done in the name of user-friendliness: provide the most commonly-used commands in a visual environment that will be friendly and approachable. Let's please reverse this misguided, ridiculous, and utterly brain-dead interface design decision:

1. Go to Tools | Customize and click the Options tab.

2. Find the Always Show Full Menus option and check it.

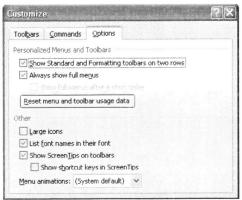

3. While you're here, consider checking Show Standard and Formatting Toolbars On Two Rows. Unless you run at high resolution, you will probably prefer using two rows. PowerPoint truncates toolbars that don't fit and arbitrarily hides icons behind an inconspicuous arrow.

We suggest you do this and leave it that way forever.

The Always Show Full Menus option is an Office-wide setting. Perform the two steps above in any Office application and it will be set across every Office application. Thank goodness for small favors...

While you're at it, head to Tools | Options, where several other choices can make your time with PowerPoint more efficient. Here is a quick tour and a few of our favorite stops:

The View Tab

Do you like your presentations to end with a black slide? We would not mind it so much if the slide were completely black, but it's not—it displays "End of Show" at the top. No thanks—we turn this one off. And if you regularly open several presentation files but don't want the Windows taskbar cluttered with them, uncheck Windows in Taskbar.

The Save Tab

We recommend turning off Allow Fast Saves and never turning it back on. This was a failed initiative to allow slower systems to save files faster by not completely rewriting the file with each Save operation. Instead, it does the digital equivalent of "tacking on to the end" any new content. This creates bloated files that are crash-prone. Today, even a 50MB presentation file saves fast; turn this one off.

If you have a specific location in which you create your presentation files, define it as the Default File Location. If you have a network of folders and sub-folders, define the top level here. I create a Drive P for all of my PowerPoint files and designate that Save and Open commands look there first, not in My Documents.

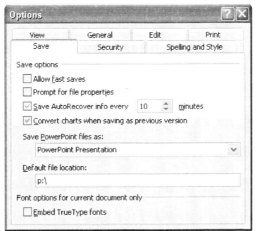

The General Tab

The important setting here is the Link Sounds value, which really should be called Link WAV files, because a WAV file is the only type of audio file for which there is any storage choice (all others are always linked, end of discussion). This threshold gives you an option of embedding the WAV file with the presentation, ensuring that the audio clip always travels with the file. We find that most users like this to be an either/or proposition and so they either set a very small number here (ensuring that all WAV files will remain external) or they set a very large number (designating that all WAV files will be embedded).

This carries potentially significant implications for those who work with audio. Embedding a large WAV file would balloon the size of the presentation file, while keeping it externally linked makes it inconvenient to transport or distribute.

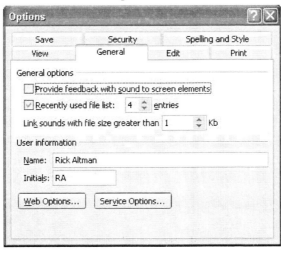

The Security Tab

Macro security is worthwhile to study for those who expect to create or receive presentation files that include VBA scripting. Password-protection is also worth understanding, as it allows you to restrict access to a presentation file. We frequently distribute presentation files that can be opened by anyone but modified only by those who know the password.

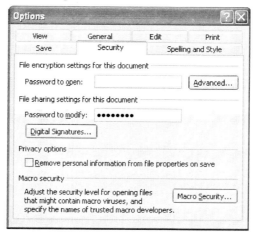

The Edit Tab

Most of these settings are self-explanatory and not earthshaking. However, if you work in a mixed environment with colleagues still using version 2000, it would be helpful and not nearly so frustrating to essentially turn off the significant features added at version XP. This also applies to a workstation that you could set up for a co-worker who goes totally overboard with exits, motion paths, and simultaneous animations: sneak onto his computer and disable New Animation Effects...

The Spelling and Style Tab
Yawn. Use as desired.

The Print Tab
How many times have you intended to print your notes or create a set of handouts but have inadvertently printed the slides themselves? I do this all the time and it steams me. Therefore, I have changed the default to print the Notes page to my black and white laser printer. I print notes much more often than I print slides, so I appreciate having that as the default.

Flying Tools

Let's start with a basic technique that works across all of PowerPoint's many toolbars and flyout menus. If you look closely at one of the toolbars on your screen, you'll notice a row of vertical dots on its left. That is an indication to you that the toolbar is portable—if you click and drag those dots, the entire toolbar will disengage and float to wherever you take it. You probably won't find a reason to move the toolbars from their position on top, but here's a handy maneuver that you might find useful:

1. Open the Draw menu from the Drawing toolbar along the bottom.

2. Click Order to open the flyout menu used for all layering and ordering of objects. Notice that it too has the row of dots.

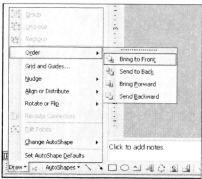

3. Click on the dots and drag the flyout away from its menu. Release the mouse and it becomes its own toolbar, floating on the slide.

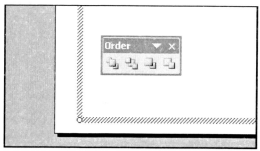

4. If you're like me, you don't like toolbars floating in the middle of your work area, so drag it down and to the right of the Drawing toolbar. It will automatically attach itself adjacent to the toolbar.

With this menu torn off and docked, ordering objects will be much, much easier—one click instead of click | click | wait for menu to appear | move mouse to desired choice | click.

This menu will remain attached in that location until you move it. Most of the flyouts off of the Drawing toolbar can be handled in this fashion:

- Align and Distribute

- Rotate and Flip

- Lines and arrows

- Other autoshapes

- Font, fill, and line attributes (these can be torn off, but not docked)

Figure 17.12 shows my Drawing toolbar, with one-click access to all of the layering and alignment commands that I use constantly.

Portable Icons

Figure 17.12
Precision placement and sequencing of objects is much easier with the tools attached to the interface.

Flyout menus are not the only elements that can relocate. In fact, just about anything that you click on can be relocated. For that you need to know the two maneuvers that unlock the interface for you:

The Alt key
Press and hold Alt while you click on an icon. When you do that, the icon becomes portable and you can move it to a different location or remove it altogether. Press and hold Ctrl at the same time and you create a copy.

The Customize dialog
Go to Tools | Customize | Commands, at which point the entire interface unlocks for you.

- Click and drag any icon from its location (you don't have to hold Alt).

- Find any command on the list and move it onto a toolbar or an existing menu. This tab of the dialog box is your gateway to every single command that exists in the application.

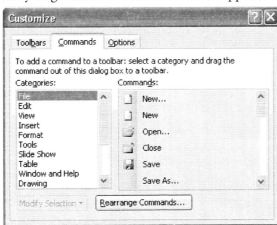

■ From the bottom of the Categories list, create a new menu entirely, attach it to the Menu, and then drag commands onto it. Notice that last command on Rick's Favorites—we'll talk about that soon.

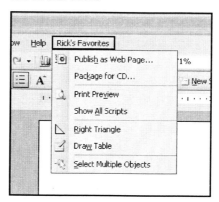

■ From the Toolbar tab of that dialog box, create a new toolbar, populate it with commands, and float or dock it anywhere you would like.

Select Multiple Objects? Did you know about that command? It brings up a dialog box showing every object on a slide, allowing you to select any of them. This is terrific when you have objects hiding behind other objects, but you've never seen that command on the standard interface; the program developers did not place it on any toolbar or menu. It lives only in the Commands list of Tools | Customize (in the Drawing category). You'll find several other commands you probably never knew existed there. Like a version history dialog, or a command to change an OLE link. View HTML source code, nudge leading—these are just a few useful commands that were left off of the interface by the developers. You can fix this.

Your Personal Litmus Test

Let's remember the premise of this chapter: it is for experienced and ambitious PowerPoint users who know what tasks they want to achieve, who know what commands they need in order to achieve them, and want quickest possible access to those commands.

Armed with the techniques discussed above, you have total freedom to place at your virtual fingertips any command you want to.

So what would you choose? What are the commands you use most often and how accessible are they? Away from the pressure of a deadline, ask yourself those questions. I'll go first:

I switch between editing the slide master and regular editing dozens of times during the initial stages of a project. The conventional steps are as follows:

1. Pull down the View menu.

2. Head down to Master.

3. Wait for a moment for the flyout to reveal.

4. Carefully head directly across to Slide Master (if I waver a bit, the flyout will close).

5. Click on Slide Master.

That fails my personal litmus test. In fact, it isn't even close! For a task as important as working on my slide masters, I want to do that with one click of the mouse. Here's how we would accomplish that:

1. Go to Tools | Customize | Commands.

2. Select View from the Category list on the left.

3. Find Slide Master from the Commands list on the right and select it.

4. Drag it onto your Standard Toolbar (the one closest to the menus).

5. If you did it right, you should see a ridiculous-looking little blob residing on your toolbar.

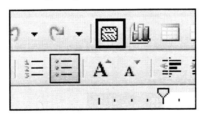

Don't even get me started on ridiculous-looking icons that bear no resemblance to any part of reality. Fortunately, that whole debate can be rendered moot:

6. With the Customize dialog box still open, right-click on the new blob—um, the icon on the toolbar.

7. Change Default Style to Text Only (Always).

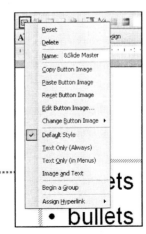

8. At your option, change the name. The optional ampersand indicates which Alt+key combination would trigger the command.

9. Close the Customize dialog and test out your new creation.

A button on my toolbar labeled Slide Master—now that passes my litmus test. Determine for yourself which commands you use most often. Create one-click access to them or place them directly onto a menu. And if you hate icons as much as I do, turn them all into text.

Optimizing Toolbar Space

If you are like me, your toolbars are going to get crowded before long. They already were crowded, and now you are adding more elements and converting them from blob to English.

Your toolbar is prime real estate: commands need to earn their way onto it. So before you go any further, scrutinize every icon that's there. Here's how my scrutiny session would go...

New: I press Ctrl+N for this command and do not need it here on my toolbar. I would send it to oblivion by pressing Alt and dragging it out onto the slide.

Open: I have Ctrl+O for that. Gone.

Save: I have been pressing Ctrl+S to save documents since WordStar 2.26 on my Osborne I in 1981. Gone.

Permissions: I have never executed this command in over 13 years of using PowerPoint.

Email: I use this command about a half-dozen times each year. I can find it on the File menu when I need it.

Print: That's Ctrl+P for me.

Print Preview: This is a potentially useful command that I often overlook. I'll tell you what I'm going to do: I'm going to put this command on probation. It can stay on my toolbar for the rest of this month. If I click it even once, it has earned itself another month. But if I haven't clicked it in that month, it's gone.

Spelling: I probably should run spell-check more. If I do, I'll find it on the menus. Where is it, somewhere in Tools?

Research: I have never clicked this and I have no idea what it is.

Cut / Copy / Paste: I use Ctrl+X, Ctrl+C, and Ctrl+V for these.

Format Painter: This is a good command and it even has a decent icon. It stays.

Undo: I use Ctrl+Z for that.

Redo: I never remember this keystroke, so the icon is useful. And because I consider Undo and Redo as sort of a package deal, I'll leave them both here.

Insert Chart: I hate charts. Gone.

Insert Table: I use this once a year. I'll find it.

Tables and Borders: Say what? Gone.

Insert Hyperlink: Once per quarter. I'll find it.

Expand All: I guess this is for outlining? I'm sure it's a perfectly fine command, but I don't outline in PowerPoint.

Show Formatting: I never knew this command existed until 15 minutes ago. It appears to show typeface and size in Outline view and on the Notes page. The day that I care what typeface is on my Notes page, I'll consider clicking this thing. Don't hold your breath.

Show / Hide Grid: This is a good command and quite useful. It stays, but can I please have something other than that barbed wire icon?

Color / Grayscale: This command stays, and I don't mind its icon.

Zoom: PowerPoint has the worst zoom controls on the planet. And as this drop down is pretty much it, I guess it stays.

Help: I don't need no stinkin' help. Kidding...I use F1 to get it.

By the time I was done, I had cleared up quite a bit of space on my Standard toolbar, the one right below the Menu line:

Figure 17.19

The Author's Perfect
PowerPoint Interface

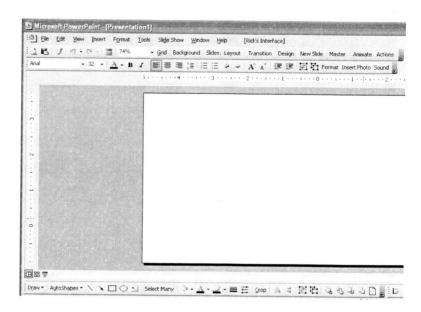

With all of that space available, I can fit many of my favorite commands and have them display in English. Big readable buttons labeled "Animation" and "Layout"—now that's a toolbar I could learn to love!

If you move an icon or a menu item a tiny bit in one direction or the other, PowerPoint creates a separator line. This is very helpful for creating logical divisions between commands.

Figure 17.19 shows the result of about 20 minutes of earnest time spent with the customization controls. Here's a brief tour:

- The bracketed menu item is a non-functioning empty menu. I use it for identification purposes: If I see Rick's Favorites up there, I know I have my preferred interface activated.

- The second item from the left on the Standard toolbar looks like the Paste command but is actually Paste Special. I recommend its use over Paste for all Clipboard elements coming from other applications.

- There are two sets of Group/Ungroup commands, as I find myself needing them when my cursor is near the top and the bottom of the screen.

- All layering, aligning, and distribution commands are available from the Drawing toolbar.

Managing Your Personal Interface

Once you get your interface just right, how do you save it, restore it, protect it, share it, and transfer it? It's not like a presentation file that you can simply save and open. PowerPoint keeps track of all of the customization work you do by storing it in a well-hidden file. It writes these changes to that file when you exit. Let's be more specific: when you exit the program *peacefully.* If you happen to crash, none of your changes will be recorded.

Therefore, when in the middle of a customization session, exit the program every ten minutes or so. This is equivalent to saving. It doesn't matter how you answer should PowerPoint ask you what you want to do with the current file. You don't care about that—just quit the application and then come right back in.

PowerPoint writes to a file that is buried in the Documents and Settings folder. Here's the path to it:

c:\Documents and Settings
   [your profile]
      Application Data
         Microsoft
            PowerPoint

Windows hides the Application Data folder by default. See our discussion in Chapter 21, page 253 about accessing this important location.

In that folder, you will find a file with a .pcb extension. If you are still using PowerPoint 2000, the file is named PPT.pcb. Those using PowerPoint XP will find a file named ppt10.pcb; PowerPoint 03, ppt11.pcb. And the new 2007, ppt12.pcb, although little of this

Not Just a Question of Speed	Creating an efficient and easily-navigated interface is about more than being productive; it's about staying healthy. Risk is quite high these days for repetitive stress injury, what with our feeling chained to our desks and pounding away at our computers for hours on end. One of the biggest risk factors is the excessive pressing of mouse finger to mouse button and the tensing of the arm muscles during same.
	Reducing the number of clicks and mousing around provides measurable relief for tired muscles.

chapter pertains to the new version (see the final section of the chapter). For the rest of this section, we will use the PowerPoint 03 filename, ppt11.pcb, but this all applies to earlier versions, also.

Treat that file like important data. Back it up, store a copy in a .zip file, move it to a different computer, send it to a colleague. Here are a few items of varying degrees of usefulness about the .pcb file:

Return to sender

If there is an active .pcb file, PowerPoint looks for it upon launch. If it doesn't find it, it starts with factory settings. So if you ever delete your .pcb file, you'll get factory settings.

Give Me Back My Interface!

At the 2005 PowerPoint Live, I played a practical joke on a co-presenter and replaced his .pcb file with one that I crafted just for him. I gave him a jump drive and told him to run the file called prep.bat. This file did the following:

1. Determined the name of his user profile and went to the folder that housed his .pcb file.

2. Backed up his current .pcb file.

3. Replaced it with the one that I created for him.

4. Launched PowerPoint, whereupon he found no toolbars, no task panes, no thumbnails, and only one menu item with one command on it.

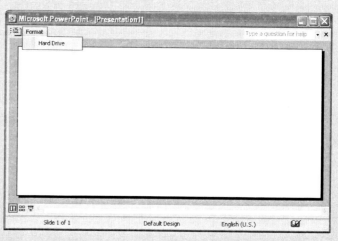

Multiple people, multiple personalities

You can keep several files in that folder—whichever file is named ppt11.pcb when the application is launched determines the look of the interface. If you want to change out your interface, you can take someone else's .pcb file or a renamed file and overwrite the current ppt11.pcb with it.

Is your computer shared among multiple users? Each can have his or her own interface file.

If you have occasion to work PowerPoint in radically different ways, you can create multiple .pcb files and shuttle them in and out. Perhaps you would want one interface for full-scale content creation, one for outlining, and another one for reviewing. After creating each interface, quit the program, find the ppt11.pcb file and copy it to, say, content.pcb, outlining.pcb, or reviewing.pcb. Then to activate any one of them, copy it over ppt11.pcb. We've seen some elaborate batch files written that ask you to pick a work environment and then activates the appropriate .pcb file before launching PowerPoint.

Do you remember your first time?

If you have never made an interface change, PowerPoint does not expect to see a .pcb file and therefore doesn't even look for it. If you were to acquire a .pcb file and put it in the correct location with the proper filename, PowerPoint would not use it on its next launch, because it thinks that there is no need for it.

So before you activate a .pcb file that you have gotten from elsewhere, make a change, any change, to the interface. Drag any icon off of any toolbar, then quit the program. The first time you make an interface change, PowerPoint wakes up, creates the .pcb file, and begins looking for it on subsequent program launches. Now you can replace it with the .pcb file that has the settings you want to activate.

We like to blow stuff up

We conducted a sadistic experiment to see how much abuse Power-Point could take. We had quite a fun time creating all sorts of "accidents":

- We deleted all of the .pcb files. PowerPoint just recreated them.

- We deleted the entire PowerPoint folder. PowerPoint didn't complain—it opened with factory settings and recreated the subfolders that it needed.

- We took the .pcb file and replaced it with nonsense files—like autoexec.bat, SexyBack.mp3, a YouTube video, and a text file that said "Mary had a little lamb" about a thousand times. PowerPoint never flinched—it ignored the file entirely and when it needed to record an interface change, it replaced the file with a real .pcb file. We were halfway disappointed.

The Downgrade that is Version 2007

We hate to end this fun chapter on a downer, but while PowerPoint 2007 reflects improvements in many areas, interface customization is not one of them. In fact, the new version takes a big step backward. Program developers are so enthused about the Ribbon and the way it has been designed, they do not want us tinkering with it.

Instead, they threw us customizers a less-than-fulfilling bone by offering the Quick Access Toolbar (QAT), a row of icons across the top of the interface. We can place any command we want there and it will hold many. But we cannot change them from icon to English and the QAT can only live in one of two locations—above the Ribbon or below it.

Hope is on the way, however. The interface has been constructed in XML and members of the development community are already hard at work creating scripts and applications to allow us to change the Ribbon and create our own Ribbon entries. These efforts will make their way to the public domain soon, and you can email us by visiting www.betterppt.com to be kept apprised.

Meanwhile, while version 2007 stood still with customization, it did not with program options, sporting a much-improved look and accessibility, not to mention several new settings that will appeal to discriminating users.

Figure 17.21 shows the integrated look of PowerPoint Options, which is activated from the Office Button, the round icon at the top-left of the PowerPoint screen. From it, you can see all file operations (and yes, Alt+F accesses it), as well as a greatly expanded list of recently-opened files.

Figure 17.21
Version 2007 enjoys a redesigned and much more accessible set of options.

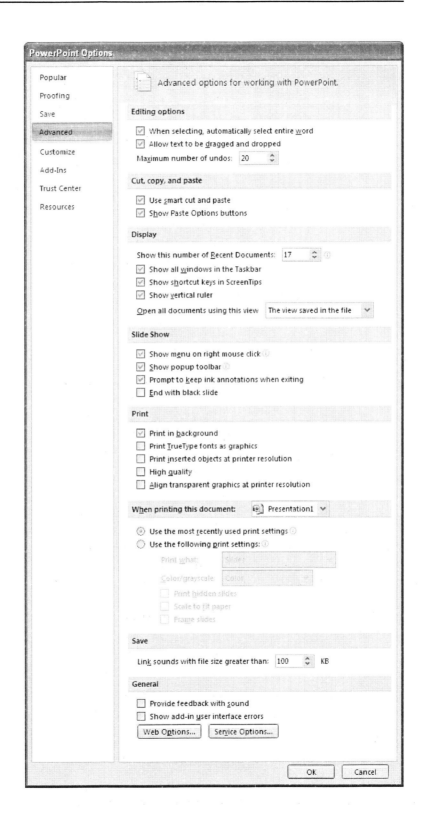

Chapter 18

Creating Intelligent Presentations

I have written a significant chunk of this book while seated in the same chair. I have begun with Chapter 1 and have written most of the book in order. I am a creature of habit and I am most comfortable when there is order to the things I do. I don't view this as unusual behavior and most people display this same tendency in one or more areas of their lives.

We're a race of linear thinkers and most of our presentations reflect that. We start at Slide 1, we end with the last slide, and we expect to advance through them in order. This is not broken and I'm not here to try to fix it. However, breaking out of that mindset is one of the most important improvements you can make as a content creator or as a presenter.

This chapter is all about how you can breathe life, flexibility, and creativity into your presentations by thinking in a non-linear way. This is an impossibly vast topic, about which entire books have been written. Like the chapter before, we'll get to fifth gear in a hurry and will be speaking to you as if you are an advanced user who knows his or her way around the program. Seat belts optional but recommended…

Click Here, Go There

The irony is not lost on me that we will work through these non-linear topics in a very linear way. The path to excellence might be circular, but the path to learning it goes in a straight line. Here are the topics we'll be discussing:

- Moving at will to a specific slide

- Jumping to a different presentation

- Opening a non-PowerPoint document

- Creating a menu-driven interface within PowerPoint

The classic example to illustrate this idea is the presentation that runs long. I'm sure this has *never* happened to you, but you've no doubt been in the audience when a presenter, we'll call her Kathleen, allows a Q&A session to run long and suddenly finds herself with five minutes left and three complete ideas still to explore. So what does she do? She flies through her slides so she can get to that final set of slides, which promises to crystallize everything she has tried to say over the last 45 minutes.

Will you remember Kathleen's dramatic and powerful close when you drive home that afternoon? Not likely—instead, you'll remember all the content she dismissed as so much slide junk as she whizzed through it. You might even wonder about a slide that looked pretty good as it flashed before your eyes, because that's the way we humans are: we're more interested in what we can't have than what we can.

Your first impression is likely to be of a person who did not completely have her act together. She became imprisoned by her own linear thinking and she paid for it.

At the core of the solution is your understanding of the basics of hyperlinking. As with a web page that offers you a way to jump somewhere else, a presentation can be programmed with this same intelligence. It's done through the Action Settings dialog, a powerful set of controls that has earned a spot on my Standard toolbar.

Any element that can sit on a slide can be programmed as a hyperlink, and Figure 18.1 shows the list of choices for standard hyperlinking. When running a presentation (i.e., when in Show mode), clicking an object programmed with a hyperlink will cause you to promptly move to the location you have set.

Figure 18.1
The hyperlink is the cornerstone of non-linear thinking.

If Kathleen had programmed a hyperlink to the first of her concluding slides, her audience might have never noticed that she was running long.

Hidden vs. Visible Hyperlinks

There are two basic methods of implementation and the one you choose is a matter of situation, preference, and even philosophy.

Roadmaps

We know many accomplished presenters who place their hyperlinks directly on the slide, in plain view of the audience, where they will never forget about them. For times when you want your audience members to see that you are making a turn onto a different street, a visible hyperlink is perfect. When I presented on this topic last year, one of my main slides looked like Figure 18.2 on the following page. Using those example buttons accomplished three important objectives:

■ It helped keep me in the flow by reminding me what to do next as I worked through a complicated set of tutorials. I was seated at the computer, in full-scale building mode, and I appreciated not having to retreat to my notes. I knew exactly what to click next to take me to the next point I wanted to make.

Figure 18.2
Visible hyperlinks are invaluable for working through complicated tasks.

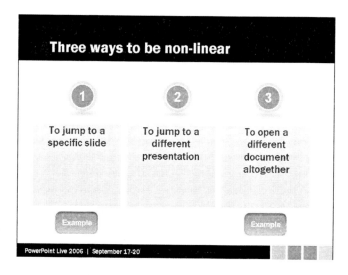

To see these hyperlinks in action, download Figure 18-02.ppt from the betterppt.com web site.

- My audience could create a visual of my progression of topics, helping them understand the concepts better.

- They could see examples of the very techniques I was teaching.

Many presenters have no reticence about showing their inner workings to their audiences, and I count myself among those who are comfortable with this way of thinking. This just says to your audience that you have given considerable thought to how you want to approach a topic. It says that you are organized.

Secret passages

Invisible hyperlinks are equally handy for those times when it is not essential that your audience members follow how you get to a certain place. This is how Kathleen would have used the technology to jump to her conclusion without anyone noticing how far behind she got.

A hidden hyperlink can take one of two forms: 1) an object that is literally invisible, devoid of fill or outline; or 2) an object that is part of the slide design. We favor the second approach, as it is all too easy to forget the location or even the existence of invisible objects. In Figure 18.2, the right-most rectangle has been programmed with a hyperlink that jumps to my last topic. If I run out of time, I can just click that rectangle and begin my conclusion. Nobody has to know about the dozen slides that I skipped over.

Flexible Intelligence

In Kathleen's case, she would have been grateful enough for a one-way ticket to her concluding slides. You, however, can build further intelligence into your slides by creating a way to return to whichever slide you were on before making the jump. Your web browser has a Back button and PowerPoint offers the Last Slide Viewed hyperlink choice.

With this hyperlink, you know you can always return to whichever slide you were on before the jump.

Hyperlinks Never Get Lost

Hyperlinks jump to specific slides in a presentation and it is important to note how PowerPoint identifies the slide. When you create a hyperlink, you identify the destination by its content, not by its position in the slide deck.

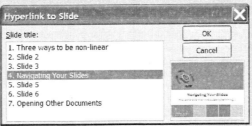

You are not creating a hyperlink to whatever slide happens to be the fourth in the deck; you identify a specific slide. If you were to move the Navigating Your Slides slide to a different place in the presentation, the hyperlink would find it just fine.

And while you identify a slide by its content, PowerPoint understands that you might change the slide's content. You can rewrite the title, change out all of the text, convert it to a chart layout, or remove all content entirely—PowerPoint will still keep the hyperlink in place.

Figure 18.5
This slide could function as home base for your presentation, and those four little rectangles at the bottom could take you to each topic.

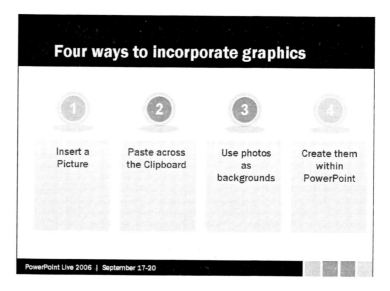

This argues for a more global view of your hyperlinking scheme, so ask yourself the following questions:

■ What are the specific slides that I might need to visit at any given time during the presentation?

■ Do I want to show my hyperlinks or not bother my audience with them?

■ If the latter, are there parts of the slide design that I could use for them?

It is unlikely that you would know the precise slide that you would be on when you wanted to employ a hyperlink, so they are best created on the slide master. One of the many reasons that I enjoyed the 2006 PPTLive conference template that Deb Shenenberg designed for us is all of those rectangles that I could use for hyperlinks!

Figure 18.5 shows a slide for a presentation on creating graphics for PowerPoint. There are four topics to be discussed and as serendipity has it, the design incorporates four small rectangles in the corner of the slide. If you were creating this PowerPoint file, you could ensure your ability to reach any of the four main topics with these steps:

1. Go to the slide master.

2. Select the first small rectangle and create a hyperlink to the slide that introduces the first main topic.

3. Select the second rectangle and make a hyperlink to the second topic.

4. Repeat for the third and fourth topics.

5. Select the long rectangle along the bottom and create a Last Slide Viewed hyperlink.

6. Select the Title placeholder (not the text itself) and create a hyperlink to the presentation's conclusion.

Now this PowerPoint file will serve you, its presenter, much more ably. No matter where you are in the presentation you know that you are one click away from any of your four main topics and from your conclusion. And if you needed to make a quick jump to one of those slides, you could go there and then return with one click.

Not all PowerPoint templates are so ideally-designed for creating hyperlinks, but we've not yet met a slide design that couldn't accommodate hyperlinking needs. Even if you were just to define quadrants of the slide—top-left takes you to the beginning, bottom-right to your conclusion—you'd be better off than being confined to a linear progression of slides.

Make sure not to obscure hyperlinks on your slide master with content on the slides themselves. If that happens, you won't be able to click on the hyperlink. Version 2007 allows you to create a custom placeholder as a hyperlink and ensure that it is always on top. With earlier versions, you need to be careful about your layering.

Nay-saying

There are three typical criticisms against the use of hyperlinks, none of which we accept:

You might accidentally click a hyperlink: Well, yes, I suppose, but so what? If you accidentally clicked anywhere on a slide, you would advance without wanting to. With your Last Slide Viewed button, you can always return with just one click.

You might forget that they're there: And you might not. What does it hurt to have them there?

Why not just use the built-in navigation: It's true that you can advance to any slide by simply typing its number and pressing Enter, pressing End to reach the last slide and Home to go to the first. But this is not nearly as good as building in your own navigation. Using the built-in navigation assumes three things that you can't really assume:

- You remember the exact number of a slide you want to go to. I never do.

- The last slide of your deck is the concluding slide that you would want to jump to. Rarely is that the case with my presentations—I usually design a conclusion slide before my thank-you-and-goodbye slide.

- Ditto for returning to the beginning of the presentation. Usually, menu-type slides that you would want to return to are not the first slide of a presentation.

If you have never tried creating your own navigation to make a presentation more flexible, you owe it to yourself to experience it.

Navigating Outside a Presentation

With the basic hyperlinking engine, you can seamlessly integrate content from outside of the PowerPoint file. You can create the following types of links:

- To other presentation files: Link to another presentation and it begins playing without delay or prompting. When that show ends, you are returned to the show and the slide that launched the second show.

- To a web page: Click on a URL link and that page opens in the default browser, as defined by your system. The presentation remains running underneath and you can Alt+Tab to it anytime.

- To any document: Any file that you can double-click on in a My Computer window can be linked to from within PowerPoint.

Click the Mouse or the Remote?

There are two factors that take the discussion deeper, and the first one is how you activate a hyperlink. Few things in the presentation business are more satisfying than watching an accomplished presenter who is adept with a wireless remote and has designed a presentation to take advantage of it. He can be all the way across the room and still command the screen. She can work the crowd, knowing just when to send her audience's attention back to a slide.

At the same time, there is quite a rush in creating a rich presentation that is full of hyperlinks and flexible navigation. Click here and go there. Click there and go here.

Hyperlinking is at its most flexible when you are able to move your mouse to objects and click them. You have as many choices as you have programmed onto a slide and you make the choice during the course of your presentation. I'm going to coin a term for this: mouse-centric navigation.

On the other hand, hyperlinking is at its most seamless when you can simply click Advance on your remote and be taken places. You make all your choices ahead of time and you advance in a linear fashion through the presentation, but with the techniques discussed in this chapter, the places you can go in that straight line can be exceptionally inventive. Another made-up term: remote-centric navigation.

Work the room or work the computer? Which approach is better?

That question has no right answer and we're not interested in inventing one. Our interest is in helping you determine when to adopt each strategy and ensuring that you get maximum value out of whichever one you choose.

In the next section, we'll create mouse-centric navigation that will make your head spin. First, let's discuss remote-centric navigation because to maximize its use, it requires familiarity with a technique that most Windows users do not explore:

Inserting Objects

An inserted object (or OLE object, for the Object Linking and Embedding engine) is different from an imported graphic or a hyperlink. An object represents the contents of a different file and can be animated in a unique way.

If you have never worked with OLE objects, you're going to need an example, so let's say that in a presentation that you're giving about home mortgage refinancing, you want to show a set of slides that graphs interest payments, called payments.ppt. You could simply import the slides into your current presentation, but the data in payments.ppt is constantly changing and you will use this data in several different presentations. When the data changes, you don't want to have to edit every presentation that uses that data; you want to update just the payments.ppt file.

Here is how you would establish this:

1. Find the precise point in your current presentation where you want to show payments.ppt. In our case here, we want it to

appear after the third bullet on this slide.

> # When is the right time to refinance?
>
> - How much principal do you carry on your first mortgage?
> - How much equity can you pull out in an emergency?
> - Have you run the numbers with the new fees?
> - Do you have the time to manage the move?

2. Those bullets are animated with a fade, the first three happening automatically, and the fourth one set to enter on a click.

3. Go to Insert | Object, click Create from File, and click Browse to find the file.

4. Locate the file and then check both Link and Display as Icon.

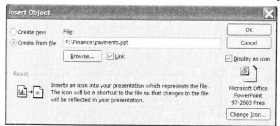

The Result section of this dialog is quite helpful. In this case, it verifies that you are creating the equivalent of a shortcut on your Desktop: an icon that represents the file. If you did not check the Link box, then PowerPoint would take the contents of the file and stuff them into the current file. This is important if you were sending the file off to someone else or posting it for distribution (all data is in one file), but not at all helpful if you want one dynamic file to be pushed out to several presentations.

If you did not check Display as Icon, PowerPoint would create a thumbnail of the first slide in the file and show that on the slide. There are plenty of times when that would be useful, and you can decide that for yourself. In this scenario, we are not interested in providing a visual cue for the hyperlink.

5. Click OK and note that a small icon appears in the middle of your slide.

6. Move the icon off the slide.

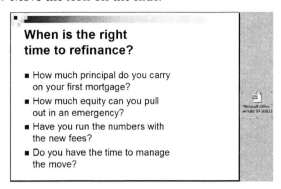

7. Open the Animation task pane, and with the icon still selected, click Add Effect. Notice that there is now a fifth choice for animation: Object Actions.

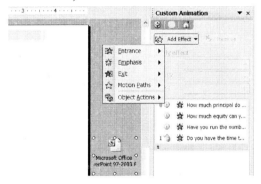

The purpose of this animation is not to determine how the object makes its appearance on the slide—it's not even on the slide, so you don't care about that. This determines what the object does when its turn comes around.

8. Click Object Actions and then Show.

9. Verify that the animation will start On Click.

10. Move the object in between the bullets so that it is fourth in line.

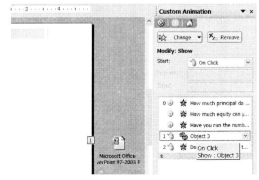

Here is a play-by-play of this slide in action:

- The title and first three bullets appear.

- You advance and the payments.ppt slide show promptly appears.

- You advance through it, and when it ends, you find yourself right back where you were.

Audience members have no idea that you ran a secondary presentation file. They just know that a relevant set of data appeared on screen to help them understand the question of interest for a refinance.

Using PowerPoint to Teach PowerPoint

At the conference, we find ourselves in an interesting conundrum: How best to use PowerPoint to show how to teach PowerPoint, while at the same time knowing that everyone is watching how we use PowerPoint and how we behave as presenters. *Paralysis of analysis* comes to mind as the operative phrase for the risk we undertake of calling so much attention to the process of presenting.

The particular challenge is how we transition from showing a presentation, which we would normally do to frame the topic and introduce the technique to be discussed, to editing a presentation, which we would need to do in order to teach the technique.

Inserted objects can help smooth and integrate this transition, because you can call for a secondary presentation to be opened for editing, instead of opened as a show. In Step 7 on page 191, choose Edit instead of Show—that will cause the PowerPoint file to be opened normally.

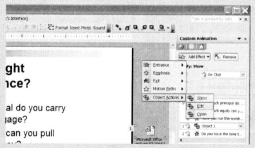

The critical requirement to this method is that the payments.ppt file continues to reside where PowerPoint originally found it. Each time you open for editing the file that contains the link, you'll be asked whether you want to update the presentation with current data. As long as you authored the presentation, it's safe to Update.

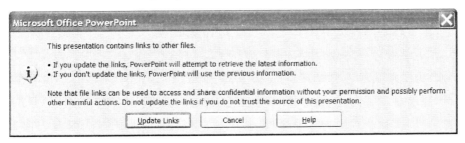

Thanks to the ability to place it in the animation sequence, this is by far the most elegant technique for running a secondary presentation

You can no longer navigate with your wireless remote—the only way to return to your primary presentation is by Alt+Tabbing back to it or by closing down the secondary presentation file. But that's okay, because the whole idea here is that you are about to actively use PowerPoint to teach an aspect of it, so you inevitably have your hand on the mouse, ready to drive.

While you are working in the secondary presentation, you'll see a Resume Slide Show icon near your Standard toolbar—that will take you back to the primary presentation.

We've found a caveat to this that is worth noting: PowerPoint normally tunes the external display correctly when you are displaying through a projector, so your audience usually sees everything correctly. But sometimes your own internal display can go bonkers when you switch back and forth between showing a presentation and editing one. To prevent this, make sure that your internal display is running at the same resolution as your external.

You can't go wrong if you set everything up for good old XGA, 1024 x 768. All components will behave well at that resolution, and even though today's equipment can run at higher resolution, your audience members and their aging eyesight might not appreciate it.

within a primary presentation. If you know when and where you want it to run, you can reduce the task down to a single click of a wireless remote or mouse. No other technique approaches this level of simplicity:

- If you created a standard hyperlink to the presentation, you would have to use your mouse to click on the hyperlinked object, requiring you or someone to be at the computer.

- If you chose to embed the presentation instead of keeping it linked, you would have to re-insert the file as an object anytime changes were made to it.

- And by dragging the icon off the slide, you make the transition completely seamless to your audience members. If instead you wanted to create a visual cue for the jump to a secondary presentation, you could choose to show a thumbnail of the slide. And if you did that, you might want to add a conventional animation to it, so that it would fade onto the slide at the right time.

Opening non-PowerPoint content

Using inserted objects is useful for just about any secondary data or application you want to show, whether it is a PowerPoint presentation or some other document. I regularly call upon PowerPoint to open Photoshop files, databases, fully-designed illustrations, even applications that take control of digital cameras when tethered by a data cable. It bears repeating and emphasizing:

Anything that can be launched from My Computer can be launched from within PowerPoint.

You would use the same procedure detailed in the sidebar on page 192:

1. Use Insert Object and Create From File.

2. Browse to the file and create a link.

3. Add an animation to it, choosing Edit as the action.

There are only two prerequisites:

- The application must be installed on the computer running the primary presentation.

- The document, if there is one, must exist.

The document…*if there is one*…hmmm…

Indeed, you don't need to open a document; you can ask PowerPoint to simply open the application. When you issue the Insert Object command, choose the other radio button, Create New, and find the program you want to run in the Object Type list. If it is there, select it and finish the process of inserting an object and including it in the animation scheme. You're done.

But what if the program is not on the Object Type list? Many installed applications do not announce their availability to the OLE engine because they do not have conventional data files associated to them. One example is iTunes. You could probably start iTunes from within PowerPoint by finding a downloaded song on your hard drive and inserting it as an object. Finding iTunes songs on your hard drive is no easy task, however, and as soon as you triggered it in the animation scheme, the song would start playing.

If the application is not readily available to you through the Insert Object dialog, you can go back to the Action Settings command and create a hyperlink to it:

1. Create an object to act as the iTunes icon (or import a graphic of its actual icon).

2. With the object selected, go to Action Settings and click Run Program.

3. Navigate through your primary hard drive to where iTunes is installed, probably under Program Files, and find the iTunes.exe file.

4. OK your way back out.

Now when you click that object, iTunes will launch.

With this technique, you cannot automatically run the program the way you can with Insert Object—this behaves like a standard

Super-Geeky Tip No. 34B: Open Any File Like a Program

If you prefer the above technique of creating a hyperlink to run a program, you can use it to open files, too. Choose Run Program from Action Settings, but before you begin looking for the file you want to open, change the file type filter from Programs (*.exe) to All Files (*.*).

Now go find your document and OK your way out. When you click the hyperlink, PowerPoint automatically launches the application that created that document and opens the file.

hyperlink, requiring you to click the object that contains the hyperlink.

▼ While attempting to launch executable files as hyperlinks, you will be stopped if your Macro Security setting is anywhere except on the lowest setting. You will be required to acknowledge the risk by answering Yes before being allowed to proceed. On the lowest setting, PowerPoint does not intervene at all.

PowerPoint as Operating System

If you regularly use PowerPoint to demonstrate or to teach, you'll find that it can function quite ably as a main platform, almost like an operating system. You could build slide masters with inserted objects and hyperlinks and create templates tuned for teaching specific skills. Coupled with navigation buttons and prompts for choosing one path or another, you can create a completely interactive, self-paced set of tutorials or demonstrations on just about any topic.

I'm not at all certain how many different types of elements can be inserted into PowerPoint and I learn about new ones almost on a daily basis. Just the other day, I discovered that the digital slide shows I create in Pro Show Producer can be run as objects within PowerPoint by finding and inserting a behind-the-scenes file. Once you understand the plumbing, you will make similar discoveries on the road toward using PowerPoint as the means by which you can open anything.

Creating Killer PowerPoint Menus

Here's the scene: you are speaking to a room of—whom would you like to be speaking to?—let's say, a group of A List Hollywood celebrities, and you are offering them advice on—what would you like to be an expert on?—let's say, you're advising them on how to better interact with the public.

Brad Pitt asks you the following question:

Brad: There's public and there's private-public. If I'm at a ballgame, I expect that I'm going to be asked to sign a few autographs. But when I'm in a small restaurant, in a corner booth, with Angelina—that's the time that I really need for my privacy to be respected.

You: That's a really good issue you raise. It's not on our agenda, but it's worth our taking a few minutes to explore.

You walk to your computer and click once. Up pops a row of topics on the top of the slide, one of which is entitled Privacy. You click it to retrieve a rich presentation of photos, quotes, and advice to celebrities who feel stalked in public.

Brad gives you a seated ovation (he stands for nobody), and other audience members are so impressed with your ability to provide this level of detail on the fly that they all text their agents and recommend your being hired as special advisor.

All this because you clicked once on a slide.

To see a video tutorial on this topic, visit www.pptlive. com/video/intelli gentpres.htm.

This fantasy was brought to you by one of the most powerful techniques that we know for infusing a presentation with flexibility and intelligence: a customizable menu that you can make appear at any time. If you can anticipate the kinds of questions that might arise during a presentation, few things are more impressive than being ready to address them.

You already know part of this solution: hyperlinks to other presentations. When done properly, the objects containing the hyperlinks are never more than one click away, and upon that click, they appear on screen, not unlike the Windows Start menu, ready to take you somewhere.

Triggering the menu

The key ingredient to this capability is the trigger: a technique whereby clicking on one object triggers the animation of another object. Figure 18.13 shows the basic mechanics of this. The rectangle

Figure 18.13
The idea of clicking one object to make another appear is central to a good menu.

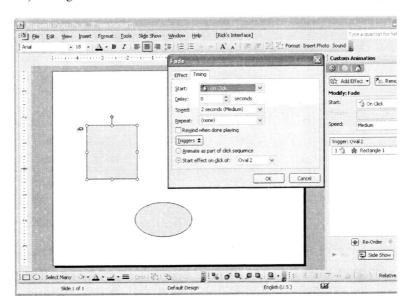

Figure 18.14
The stage is set for
this menu: room for
it top-right, and
rectangles to act as
triggers lower-right.

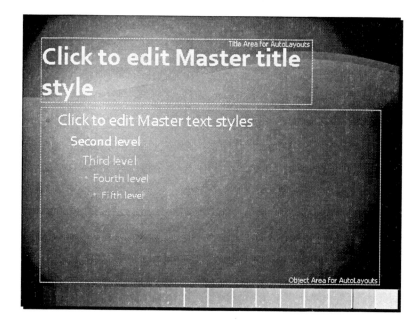

has been given a fade, set to appear On Click. The question is what click? The answer comes from the Timing dialog of the rectangle's animation, where we have instructed the animation to take place when we click the oval.

Click the oval and see the rectangle. That's the basics of a trigger.

As with a standard hyperlink, the idea is to find a design element on the slide and make it be the trigger for the menu. Once the menu appears, standard hyperlinks take over. Here is how we would build one for our Hollywood audience.

First off, the whole idea of this menu is that it be just one click away, anytime, anywhere. That means that it must be built on the slide master, and Figure 18.14 shows the one controlling the design and the animation for this presentation. The rectangular quadrants along the bottom provide a good opportunity to create triggers, and we have shortened the size of the title placeholder to accommodate the menu's appearance at the slide's top-right corner.

I do not like the look of hyperlinks applied to text (they get under-lined and they change color, just like the old-style web-page hyperlinks in the 1990s). Therefore, I take on a bit of extra work when I create hyperlinks for text strings: I create invisible rectangles over the text and apply the hyperlinks to them.

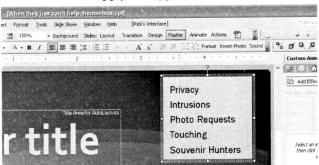

Creating the text is easy—in this case, it's just a string of five short items. Notice that I am zoomed way in, 150%, as is my standard practice for performing precision placement on a slide. Once the text is in the correct position, I create the rectangles, apply the hyperlinks to them, and remove their fills and outlines.

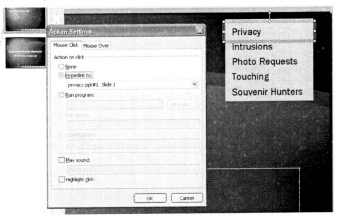

▼ If you expect to deliver this presentation with the PowerPoint Viewer, do not make the trigger object completely invisible (they become unclickable when run from the Viewer. Instead, pick a fill color and set it to be 99% transparent. It will not appear on screen, but the Viewer will recognize it. For more on the Viewer, see Chapter 21.

Once I have drawn and positioned the rectangles and created their hyperlinks, it's time to animate them. So I drag a marquee around the text and each of the invisible rectangles, and apply a fade, Very

Fast, to all of them at once. I set the first one to start On Click and leave the others to start With Previous.

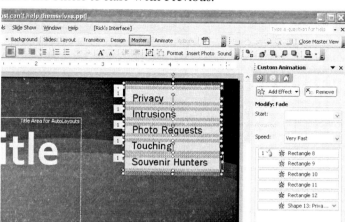

With each of the animations in the task pane still selected, it's time to create the trigger, using the Timing dialog. But first I must know the name of the object that's going to act as the trigger. PowerPoint does not make this easy on me, as the only time that an object's name appears is when you animate it. So I must scroll down to the bottom of the slide, select the rectangle I want to use, and then apply a temporary animation to it, just so I can get its name. It's called Rectangle 23.

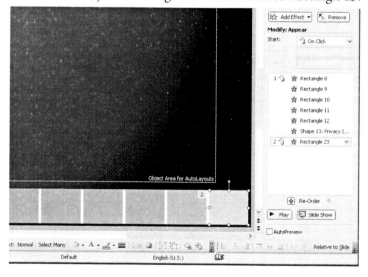

Once done, I promptly remove the animation and get back to business. I select all six animations, right-click, choose Timing, click

Triggers, and then choose Rectangle 23 as the object that will start the animation.

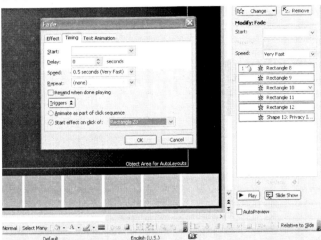

To make the effect a bit more refined, I also create an exit fade for the menu, and trigger it to the adjacent rectangle (which is Rectangle 24, I checked). This way, I can reveal the menu by clicking one of the rectangles and hide it by clicking the other.

Finally, I apply a 35% transparency to the text string so it sinks into the slide background a bit.

Letting go of our Brad Pitt fantasy, however reluctantly, you can use this technique successfully if you have any inkling at all about related topics that might be raised in a presentation. These would be questions not quite germane enough to be part of your main talk, but worthy of discussion should your audience ask.

Design your main slide master so it can accommodate a block of text and then think of five or six topics that you might be asked about during the presentation. Prepare short slide decks for each one, with a few simple idea points about them, just enough to get you started, and hyperlink to them. Your audience will be impressed beyond belief—chiefly with your ability to anticipate their questions, but also with a technique within PowerPoint that they will probably have never seen before.

Over the course of a four-day PowerPoint conference, I can think of about 10 topics that are sure to come up at one point or another. You can download a .zip file containing my collection of linked presentation files as pptlive.zip from the betterppt.com web site.

Trainer Heaven

The techniques uncovered in this chapter can be put to great effect in countless situations. Of all the strategies discussed throughout this book, the ones in this chapter carry the greatest potential of taking you to an altogether different plain of proficiency as a presenter or as a content creator.

And if I had to identify one group in particular that would benefit the most, it would be those who use PowerPoint as a training tool. The demands put upon students learning from a PowerPoint presentation are different than with an audience listening to a sales pitch or a keynote address. In short, the demands are much higher. They need to pay closer attention to details, they usually take many more notes, they are often following along with their own notebooks, and if they are learning a software program, are likely to be watching smaller elements on screen, like icons, tools, and menus.

As the trainer, this increases your burden, also. You have to minimize extraneous screen activity, avoid being herky-jerky with the mouse, eliminate unnecessary dialog boxes and windows that are not relevant to the task.

You can achieve all of that with effective use of hyperlinks, linked objects that automatically open data files, visual cues, and interactive menus. These are the ingredients to a cleaner and more enjoyable experience, both for you and for your students.

Chapter 19

Fabulous Photos

We'd like to start this chapter by saying that we're in favor. We're in favor of photos. Big photos, huge photos, bright photos, loud photos—the bigger, huger, brighter, and louder the better.

At the same time, it's not like photos need defending. I sense no bum rap that they suffer through or a bad reputation they have to live down. In fact, ask anyone who has had to sit through an endless procession of bad bullets—they would kill for a slide with a photo on it. Even a bad photo.

Except in the context discussed back in Chapter 4, Bitter Backgrounds, photos are not misunderstood in this regard...but they are misunderstood. And they are loved and appreciated. So consider this chapter a primer on all that you need to know and all that you need to forget with respect to using photos in your presentation files.

Resolution Confusion

Are you ready to hear the most widely-circulated misunderstanding concerning photos into PowerPoint? Here it is:

> **When imported to PowerPoint, a 300-dpi photo will look better than a 72-dpi photo.**

This is an incorrect statement. In fact, two photos of the same dimension (let's say 1024x768), one exported at 300 dpi, one exported at a lower resolution, will look exactly the same and will have the *exact same file size*.

One reason that you're probably shaking your head in the general direction of my book right now is because most software programs have misled you all these years. They have allowed you to speak the language of the print industry while working with display technology.

Get the dot out of here!

What exactly does it mean to have a photo appear on your screen that is 300 dots per inch? You might be able to explain to me the part about the dots, but an inch? What's an inch? On the monitor that's seated on my lap right now (yes, while my wife sleeps and my dog sneezes...still), an inch is over 7% of the total width. When this same image is projected before my audience, an inch would be less than .01% of the width. Same image, same computer, same photo, very different inch.

▼ Before you resize photos, make copies so you preserve the original fidelity. See page 213 for details.

Measuring in inches has absolutely no meaning when discussing an image on screen, and therefore the term for resolution known as dots per inch is equally irrelevant. The dot refers to an actual placement of ink or toner on a printed page and that page has a measurable size. You really can measure how many dots of ink fit within one inch when you are printing.

We can do no such thing when we are discussing a photo that appears on screen, because there is no such thing as a dot and there is no such thing as an inch. There are only pixels—the basic unit of measure on a computer screen, the single grid point in an image, the abbreviation for "picture element."

Figure 19.1

Measuring the dpi value of a photo being saved in pixels is meaningless and confusing.

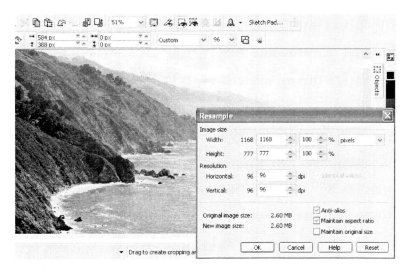

The only measurement that is relevant with respect to the quality of a photo being prepared for PowerPoint is its size in pixels—1024 pixels wide...800 pixels wide...600 pixels deep, etc. This is why software that implies otherwise, as we see in Figure 19.1 does us all a disservice.

This application here is just one of many programs that commits this error. If you were to adjust the dpi value in this dialog box, the software would compensate by changing the image size. This is tantamount to two wrongs making a right: when sizing a photo for Power-Point, the only thing that matters is its size in pixels. If the image were destined for a magazine and were being measured in inches, that would be different.

Think Pixels

Let's start by making this really simple, so if you get fed up with this chapter right now, you'll already have the important part:

> **Size your photos for 1024 pixels of width
> or 768 pixels of height.**

Over 90% of all presentations delivered today are projected at XGA resolution—1024 pixels across by 768 pixels deep. If your landscape photo is sized at 1024 pixels wide or your portrait photo at 768 pixels high, you guarantee its fidelity when projected full screen. You'll be exercising overkill for photos less than full screen, but the increase in the file's size is utterly insignificant. If you deliberately decrease the size of your photo because you don't intend to use it full-screen, Murphy's Law will immediately activate, your design will change, and

Figure 19.2
PowerPoint suffers from inchitis, also.

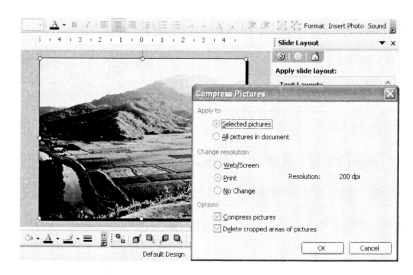

you'll need it full screen. Just keep it at that size, even if you're using it smaller.

This discussion assumes that you have control over the size of the photo, but many times you don't. Like when you get sent a 150-pixel wide thumbnail and you're expected to do something with it. As soon as you take the dpi nonsense out of the equation, you can think rationally about this and reach an intuitive solution:

You must display it in PowerPoint at a small size!

And how do you know what size to make it? How can you size it to 150 pixels? You can't, because PowerPoint is brain-dead this way, also! Look at Figure 19.2 and you'll see that PowerPoint insists on measuring this photo in inches.

Figure 19.3
This photo was taken by an 8.1 megapixel camera, a typical resolution by 2007 standards.

▼ For more detail on the resolution misconception, visit the PPTFaq site and read www.pptfaq.com /FAQ00075.htm.

Fortunately, you are operating in a very forgiving medium. It really doesn't take a lot to make a photo look good on a computer display or out of a projector. You don't have to worry about color-matching, trapping, registration errors, CMYK conversions, or any of the issues that send those in the print business to early retirement. If it looks good on your screen, there's a good chance it will look good when projected or shown. If you can test it out on the ultimate output device, so much the better.

Welcome to the Better PPT Photo Lab

Figure 19.3 is a photo of my two daughters outside on a sunny fall day in San Francisco. It was taken with my Canon EOS XT, a digital camera that takes photos at 8.1 megapixels.

Dimension	3456 pixels wide
	2304 pixels high
Filesize	3.3MB

When imported into PowerPoint, it is such a large photo that my older daughter's head barely fits on the slide. In Figure 19.4, we have superimposed the size of the actual slide so you can get a sense of how large the photo is. The slide thumbnail on the left will give you the same indication.

Figure 19.4
When imported to PowerPoint, this photo is many times larger than the slide itself.

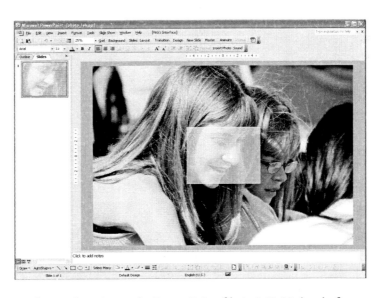

With just this photo, the PowerPoint file is 3.5MB, but before you go on auto-pilot and conclude that it needs to be shrunk down before import, or by PowerPoint after import, consider this:

▓ You could use this photo in one of countless ways, including an extreme close-up.

▓ You could zoom in or pan and maintain total fidelity

If these techniques sound appealing, you'll want to keeping your photos at full resolution. More on that later—now let's experiment...

At 1024 pixels wide...

In order to follow our own advice above—size photos for 1024 pixels of width or 768 pixels of height—we have taken the photo into an image editing program (Photoshop, PhotoPaint, Paint Shop Pro, ACDSee, et al) and reduced it in size to 1024 x 682 (we told it to size the width to 1024 and allow the height to adjust in proportion).

▼ Download photo_lab.ppt from the betterppt.com web site for a complete analysis and recap of the experiments discussed in this chapter.

The result is a photo that looks perfect when displayed at full-width and yet is a fraction of the size of the original: 254KB.

For 90% of you, this photo will now be completely usable in every scenario you might think of, from full-slide down to thumbnail. Our unofficial surveys show that about 10% of you might want to go with a tight shot, like the extreme close-up shown above, and it is those people who will be disappointed with the results. Even on the black and white pages of this book, I'll bet you can see the difference between the 1024-wide image below and the full-resolution one on the opposite page.

Look at her hair, the texture of her skin, and the eyelashes. Whatever differences you see here, shown three inches wide and in grayscale, multiply many-fold for color output on a high-resolution display.

Once you size the photo down to 1024 pixels of width, you close the door on close-ups like this. There are no longer enough pixels in the photo to provide the detail needed.

At 800 pixels wide...
We see almost no difference than if we were looking at the 1024-pixel wide image. That suggests to us that the relationship between resolution and file size is not linear. We saved a bundle of file space in the first decrease in size, but not nearly so much this time: only 70K, down to about 185K. Even sized up full-slide, this one looks almost identical to the 1024-pixel-wide photo.

At 640 pixels wide...
When displayed at full-slide width, you can clearly see that this photo does not have as much detail. Given that you're only saving about 40K (file size of 144K), sizing down to 640 pixels or lower seems pointless.

Figure 19.8
One of these photos
is 3.5MB in size and
the other is 104K, but
at this size, you
wouldn't be able to
determine which
is which.

Figure 19.8 shows the four resolutions that we worked with in this little experiment, and displayed at this small size, I'll defy you to see a difference. On my 24-inch display, I have to practically touch my nose to the screen to discern the subtle differences in Erica's lashes.

But in Figure 19.9, it's a different story altogether, as once again, the demands of such a tight zoom are too much for the versions of this photo that have been reduced in size. The other scenario in which lack of resolution shows up is with a sweeping pan across a photo, available for you to see if you download photo_lab.ppt. An effective pan requires that the photo start out significantly larger than the slide

Figure 19.9
Close-ups like these
expose the photos
that have given away
too many of their
pixels.

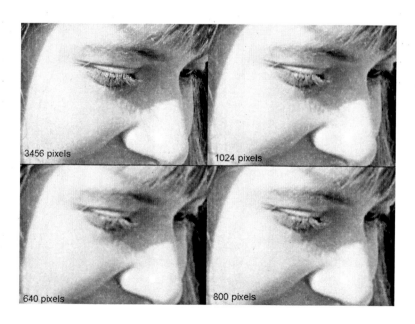

itself, and that spells trouble for photos that are only the size of the slide or smaller.

Am I recommending that you not downsize your photos? If so, I'm sure it wouldn't be the first time that I have contradicted my own advice across the pages of this book, but it would probably be some sort of record to have done it within the same chapter.

No, I'm not necessarily advising you to become a glutton with your photos, and there is no question that if you needed to distribute a presentation or make it available for download, you would want to do everything possible to keep the size down.

I can only speak for myself. When I have a rich presentation to prepare that I know will be run on my own computer, I do not resize my photos. I don't care how large my PowerPoint file becomes, but I do care about having every possible creative option available to me. Pans and zooms are standard operating procedure when I'm hoping to evoke emotion with a photo montage and for those two maneuvers, I need every last pixel.

On some computers, there might be a drop in performance with photos this large, but on any of the desktops or notebooks that I have purchased since 2003, I notice none whatsoever.

Managing the Move

Should you choose to get aggressive with the size of your rich presentation files, there are three courses of action available to you:

- Resize your photos with image-editing software before importing them to PowerPoint.

- Let PowerPoint do it for you, with the Compress Pictures command.

- Use third-party software that compresses the entire Power-Point file.

If you have a preferred image-editing application, you not only know how to size a photo, you've probably done it countless times already. For those with less experience, I recommend picking up a copy of ACDSee, the versatile image viewing, organizing, and editing tool from www.acdsystems.com. With a buy-in starting at $40, you get a handy array of tools and a friendly interface, as shown in Figure 19.10. I own Photoshop, PaintShop Pro, and PhotoPaint, and yet I often reach for ACDSee for quick crops, format conversion, and changes in size, thanks to the program's quickness and accuracy.

Part Four: Working Smarter

Figure 19.10
ACDSee proves to be
a handy investment
for anyone who
works ambitiously
with photos.

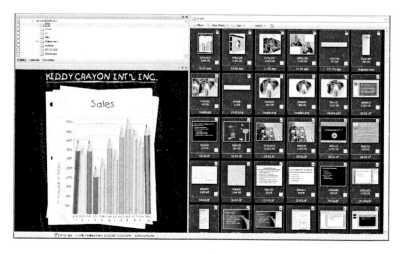

PowerPoint has its own built-in compression function, available for any selected photo (via the Picture toolbar or the Format Picture dialog) or for every photo (using the Tools drop-down in the Save As dialog).

This procedure works according to algorithms that nobody has satisfactorily explained to me. Sometimes it reduces the size of a file by many factors and other times it does nothing. And as mentioned earlier, PowerPoint muddles the whole dot-per-inch/pixel situation, associating web quality with 96 dpi.

▼ In versions 2003 and earlier, you cannot compress photos that have been placed into a shape. With version 2007, you can.

Still, it doesn't hurt anything and is worth trying when you need to keep file sizes down and when you don't anticipate using photos that are larger than the slide itself.

As for after-market tools for file compression, we like NXPowerLite from the London-based Neuxpower company. For $45, you get an easy-to-use utility that takes care of business with no backtalk. And wow, does it work—our photo_lab file went from 3.9MB to 850K with no discernible picture loss. At PowerPoint Live 2006, company reps flew all the way to San Diego and gave every single patron a free copy. www.neuxpower.com.

Steve Rindsberg and his PPTools suite of programs offer an optimizer, among many other useful PowerPoint utilities, and you can find out about them at www.pptools.com.

We also like Microsoft MVP Bill Dillworth's SizeMe utility, which reports in detail on what might be responsible for your file bloat. http://billdilworth.mvps.org.

Protect Originals

The most important part of this whole process is insuring against your reducing the heck out of your photos without having originals tucked safely away. If you find yourself in Photoshop about to downsize an image, take a moment and save the file in native .psd format. Ditto for PhotoPaint and a .cpt file. Once you do that, then size it down and export it to whatever format you want.

We know how easy it is to forget to save photos in native formats, and that's why we like the post-production compression tools such as NXPowerLite. Reducing images once they are already in PowerPoint removes all risk to the original photos.

Digital Photo Survival Skills

If digital photography does not prove to be the killer app of this decade, it means that something really huge is coming tomorrow. Using a digital camera, even an inexpensive one, is a liberating experience for so many reasons beyond the fact that it is much, much cheaper than using film. Here are a few of the dozens of reasons why digital photography has become one of the most popular pastimes for anyone who likes taking photos:

A digital camera makes you a better photographer: Even if we're just talking dumb luck here, we take so many more photos of a given scene than we ever would have before, one of them is bound to be good. Furthermore, you get instant feedback through your LCD and that helps you develop an eye for what works and what doesn't. Waiting three days and relying on memory never worked for me across three decades of using film cameras; I learned more about composing shots in one year of using digital.

A digital camera makes your subjects better models: I've observed that people are willing to pose for about three shots; after that, they begin to ignore you. Start snapping, my friend, because that's when you'll get some really good shots.

If you are paying for film, you are likely going to take only one or two shots of friends or family, and they're probably going to pose for you, like these photos here:

But if you know that you've got 120 shots left on your 1GB card and you can delete bad shots moments after taking them, you're going to shoot more. And when you do, your subjects are going to get tired of smiling for you. That's when you start to get photos like these:

Traditionalists are welcome to disagree, but to my eye candid photos tell more about somebody. On the left is a father and his adopted daughter, for whom he went to hell and back when she was just months old. They are very close and the quiet moment they share in the second photo conveys that. On the right are my daughter and my sister and they are best friends and confidants. That comes through much more in the non-posed shot.

You can fix your foul-ups: There are entire books on this subject, and the world of photo-refining can be an intimidating place. Coming soon will be some tips that anyone can follow for making better photos.

Whether they are your own photos or ones supplied by others, understanding the basics of photo taking, exposure, focusing, and cropping will make your presentation content that much stronger. Here are a few topics to consider...

Depth of Field

Even today's point-and-shoot cameras are capable of manipulating light to affect how a camera focuses. On a bright day, you can really learn a lot about this, because you have a lot of room to adjust. These two photos were taken just 10 seconds apart:

The one on the left was taken with a slow shutter speed, and to compensate, the camera closed ("stopped down") the lens by a considerable amount. This results in a greater focal length ("depth of field"). The photo on the right underwent the reverse: very fast shutter speed which caused the lens to open much wider. That results in a much shorter focal length. You can see all the way across the street in the left photo but you can barely see five inches past the flowers on the right photo.

If you need a photo to be descriptive, the greater depth of field would serve you well. If you want to be dramatic, the shorter depth of field is what you want.

Figure 19.15
If you did not blur out the background when you took the photo, you can do it with software.

If you didn't do this out in the field, the digital darkroom can help you in one direction. While making a blurry photo sharp is next to impossible, going the other direction is possible. It requires proficiency with your image editor's selection tools. With them, you can isolate the background and make it blurry. That helps bring focus and drama to the foreground.

Figure 19.15 shows a photo undergoing such a transformation. The coach has been "masked" (appearing in these pages as a white glow around him). This allows us to work on just him or just the background. In this case, the coach was unaltered and the background behind him underwent a "Gaussian Blur," so named for the mathematician who developed the algorithm two centuries ago.

Zoom

There is nothing like a good telephoto lens to allow you to sneak up on people and get good candid shots. A good zoom feature on your camera also lets you alter reality. Witness these two photos, both taken from the exact same position.

With a normal 35mm lens (left), you get a good sense of the distance between the foreground tree and the background tree. A telephoto lens tends to shrink the observable distance between foreground and background and the 300mm lens used on the right gives the impression that you can practically touch the tree in the back.

As with a short focal length, zoom can add energy and emotion to a photo, but it does so at the expense of realism. If you need your photo to be accurate, use a normal lens.

The most important thing to know about zoom is to avoid "digital zoom" at all costs. If your camera offers it, scroll the menus until you find out how to disable it. If a camera you are considering for purchase makes a big deal about it—if that's the best feature they have to advertise—run away fast! To reiterate:

Avoid using your camera's digital zoom!

Optical zoom uses the lens itself to bring the subject closer—the physical elements of the lens move in order to change the field of vision. Digital zoom does nothing more than enlarge a portion of the image using an interpolation that has nothing to do with making the image better. Only bigger.

This is similar to what you could do using the crop tool of your image editor, with one important difference: your software is much better at it than the camera is.

Figure 19.17 is a photo taken at the maximum level of optical zoom. It is a sharp, focused image taken with a 5MP point-and-shoot camera.

In order to zoom in even more on the oranges—in PowerPoint, in another application, or in a print—you have two choices: 1) use your camera's digital zoom; or 2) crop this photo and then enlarge the remaining area. While it's easier to push a button on your camera than work the photo with software, the results aren't even close.

Figure 19.17
If you wanted to get a closer look at these oranges, there is a right way and a wrong way to do it. Digital zoom would be in that second category.

The photo on the left is a product of 30 seconds spent in ACDSee or with PowerPoint's own tools: I simply cropped the photo tighter and then enlarged it. The one on the right is my camera's pathetic attempt to do the same thing. Turn off digital zoom and pretend you never heard of it.

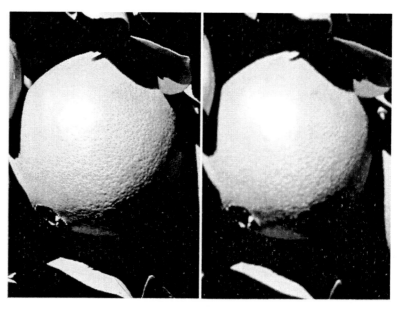

Flash and exposure

This one's easy, right? You use it when you are indoors and you turn it off when you are outdoors.

What if I told you that you might have better results if you were to do the exact opposite? Using a flash indoors tends to overpower the existing light, creating bright and often harsh images. If you can shoot without flash, the natural light of a room tends to be warmer. Please forgive the poor composition of these photos, with the lights of the menorah right in front of these girls' faces, but they illustrate the point well.

On the left, the candles are overwhelmed by the flash and the granite counter looks cold and harsh. But on the right, the scene is captured more realistically—the candles were the only illumination at the time. You see their reflections in the countertop and the warm glow they give to the faces. Getting this shot required a steady hand (much slower shutter speed) and a bit of digital work to bring up the midtones, but the effort was worth it.

Meanwhile, a nice bright summer day, with the sun directly overhead, could spell death for your ability to capture facial features. Witness these photos of a nice Yosemite hike at Vernal Fall:

All of that rushing white water in the background captured the lens's attention (left), and everything else was underexposed. But with the addition of flash (right), that provided just enough light to cut through all of that glare.

Outdoor flash is much more subtle—you rarely have to worry about it looking artificial, as you do indoors. It just provides a bit of illumination to fight backlighting and dark shadows from midday sun. The auto-husband removal is an optional feature, usually costing extra.

The risk of shooting indoors without a flash is that your images will be blurry. As the camera struggles to get enough light, it slows down the shutter considerably, amplifying any bit of shake you might introduce. You can help by telling the camera that it doesn't have to try so hard to get sufficient light. Find your camera's exposure setting and reduce it, effectively telling it that it is okay if the image is a bit dark. With that requirement eased, it will use a faster shutter speed, allowing you to take sharper photos.

And what about those dark photos? While it is very difficult to save a photo that has been overexposed, you would be amazed at how much information can be squeezed out of an underexposed shot.

I promise that I did no doctoring to these photos other than what we're about to describe. The photo on the left is exactly how my 10-year-old daughter took it, from inside a mission where flash photography is prohibited. The photo on the right was the result of increasing the image's midtones. It took 30 seconds in ACDSee.

Moral of the story: Don't be afraid to underexpose photos, and don't give up on dark photos.

A load of crop

The single most important difference you can make with your photos is to remove parts of them. You play an important editorial role when you make decisions that help focus attention and bring more energy to a scene. We have so many examples of this, we have prepared a download for you, but we'll share one of them here in these pages.

Figure 19.22 is a typical example of a tourist or vacation photo, with the subjects placed right in the center of the shot and a bunch of noise in the background. Like we really need an ugly picnic table and iron barbecue back there?

Download cropping.ppt for an interactive tour of many photos made better with the right crop.

Most amateur photographers place their subjects in the center and probably will until the day they die. Fortunately, the digital age allows you to make your creative decisions after the fact, and Figure 19.23 shows the result of a simple crop. With the unattractive part of the background out of the picture, the truly beautiful part that is the Santa Barbara coastline becomes more prominent. And just by putting the two people a bit off to one side, the photo becomes vital and more interesting.

This is not difficult at all to do in PowerPoint, especially if you create better access to the Crop tool. The hardest part is remembering to

Figure 19.22
This photo suffers from unimaginative composition and too many visual distractions.

Figure 19.23
Twenty seconds with a crop tool and now this photo is ready for a frame.

think about it, instead of just accepting a photo's default placement. It's a matter of thinking asymmetrically: *If I moved this person out of the center of the photo, would it look better? If I moved part of her off the slide, what would that do?*

The before and after examples on these facing pages are quite telling. Otherwise plain layouts give off completely different feelings with the help of simple crops. I also like that the subjects in the photo end up being bigger.

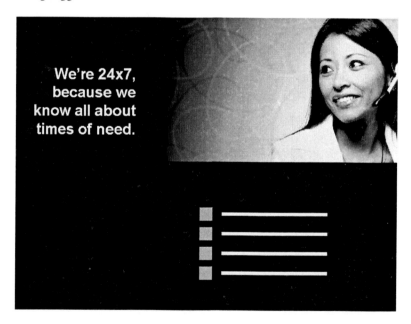

Figure 19.26
Cute girl...nice
message...

I probably use the Crop tool in PowerPoint more than any other this side of animation and layering. I was gratified to discover that if I used the Customize dialog to ask for an English-speaking button instead of an icon, and I labeled it &Crop, I could activate it with Alt+C. I have cut way down on my mousing around by moving the cursor to the photo, pressing Alt+C to activate the tool, and then being able to begin cropping right away.

Figure 19.27
Cute girl...nice
message...powerful
visual!

As you can tell, I love my digital cameras...all six of them. I still have my first one, a 1MP box that Kodak introduced in 1995 for $800. As far as I know, it was the first digital camera made available in this country. When we used it at the 1996 CorelWorld User Conference (www.corelworld.com) to take photos and then, 10 minutes later, projected them in the main ballroom, it was nothing short of a miracle.

I am never satiated. At this very moment, my auction software is poised to make an eBay bid on Canon's newest model of digital SLR. I'll let you know how it goes in the next chapter.

Digital photography is truly one of the happiest addictions I have ever had...

Chapter 20

Music and Video: Looking Beyond PowerPoint

We're sure you've heard the expression before, or a derivation: "When all you have is a hammer, everything looks like a nail." It describes our human desire to make things work, even if they are not destined to.

We have seen some amazingly deft and inventive workarounds to overcome PowerPoint's shortcomings and we applaud the ingenuity of those who refuse to give up.

Nonetheless, there are times when the wisest course of action is to acknowledge that PowerPoint is merely a tool designed to help you perform tasks. And for some tasks, it is the wrong tool. This chapter addresses a niche that is exploding before our eyes—multimedia and video. And with it explodes the illusion that PowerPoint can handle all of our multimedia needs.

Beyond Slides

We have noticed two clear trends over the last few years of hosting the PowerPoint Live User Conference. The first is a growing desire to deliver content on DVD, and the second is an affinity for creating movies, be they promotional videos for business purposes or family videos commemorating significant lifecycle events. Family keepsake videos are big; I have literally formed a secondary business around it.

These two areas of interest share many challenges and rewards, not to mention an entire cottage industry and software niche. They also share the inescapable conclusion that PowerPoint is not the right tool to use.

Would that the Package for CD function contain the magic necessary to convert your PowerPoint presentations into a digital video stream that could be ripped directly to DVD. The cold truth is that there is no easy way—only circuitous, multi-step routes—to convert a PowerPoint presentation into a DVD video.

The more glaring issue is the set of deficiencies that work against you when trying to create an evocative slide show to move or persuade an audience. To wit:

- Unreliable synchronization of music to imagery
- No support for fading an audio clip
- Inconvenient handling of photos
- Limited support for playing video
- Poor timeline
- Inability to combine or script zooming and panning

None of these shortcomings is addressed in PowerPoint 2007, and many of us who have cut our teeth using PowerPoint to create digital video are now looking at other applications that are better suited to these tasks. You can spend as little as $50 or as much as $1,700 in the software niche that doesn't really have an agreed-upon name yet. Some vendors refer to their programs as digital video creation tools; others as home movie makers. Some call this photo slide show creation; others prefer the more impressive digital production and post-production.

The least sexy phrase is the one that has caught on: non-linear editing. NLE software allows you to slice and dice video and move from the beginning to the end of a movie with one command. VHS is linear; movie-making software is non-linear.

By any name, these programs all offer the following critical set of features:

External referencing of photos: Instead of trying to import and digest megabytes worth of imagery, these programs store references to the external files. Any changes made to the source files are instantly reflected in the project, and you needn't worry about downsampling the photos first to keep file sizes down. That is one of your export choices so you can wait until the very end to determine the resolution and quality of your movie.

Complete audio-video synchronization: No matter where you are in a movie's timeline, you can confidently match an audio clip to the imagery behind it. If you want to cut to your Niagara Falls panorama right at the crescendo of Beethoven's Fifth or when Kelly Clarkson hits a high note, that's no problem, and you can test it by playing just that slide. (In PowerPoint, you would have to start the slide show on the first slide that the music begins on in order to even hear the music.)

Built-in facilities for editing audio: PowerPoint requires that you edit your audio clip before importing it. Most, if not all, digital video software allows you to fade and trim imported audio, making it much easier to refine your timings.

Support for video: These programs make very little distinction between still photos and motion video. If it's a standard format, like TIF, BMP, JPG, AVI, MPG, WMV, they will accept the file and play or display it.

Direct export to most standard video formats and built-in DVD creation: Again, PowerPoint knows no such capability. Migrating a PowerPoint slide show to video involves one of two routes: 1) Using after-market software that converts it to Flash, and if that's not your desired format, going from there to MPG, AVI, WMV, or MOV along a very bumpy route; or 2) Using a program like Camtasia Studio to make a real-time recording of your slide show and save it to a video file. Only then can you burn a DVD. You can be 75% into this process and still be wondering, with good reason, if you shouldn't chuck the whole thing and start over in a different authoring tool.

Creating or Burning?

If you are primarily interested in collecting video, photos, or other data and preserving them on a DVD's 4GB of elbow room, then you have a multitude of software choices, ranging from $30 for a shareware program you can pick up on download.com to $300 for a full-featured menu-creation and quantity-burning application. These programs offer little in the way of creativity – you are expected to already have your content created and ready to be burned.

Most creative professionals will have little need for burn-only programs, because the software designed for content creation usually includes sufficient DVD-burning capability. At the top of the mountain is Adobe's Production Studio Creative Suite, geared for those who work regularly with video (as opposed to mostly with still photography). This behemoth package could keep chiropractors in business for years, offering Premiere Pro, Photoshop, Illustrator, After Effects (a dedicated object animation tool), Encore (for creating menu-driven DVDs), and Audition (a full-featured audio-editing package). This bundle retails for $1,699.

When you pull yourself off the floor, we'll talk about the alternatives that cost a fraction of that price. Many of you already have some flavor of Photoshop or a similar image-editing program, and Corel-Draw users don't need to purchase an image editor because they get PhotoPaint in the box. If you need a program like Illustrator for vector-drawing work, you probably already have one of those, too. You can pick up a very good audio-clip editor for free (WavePad at www.nch.com.au/wavepad), and the slimmed-down Elements version of Premiere is a much more digestible $99.

Premiere is vintage Adobe: it is chock full of features hiding behind an impossibly vast array of toolbars, icons, and other interfaciala. If you already speak Adobe, you'll be comfortable with either flavor of Premiere; if not, then even the $99 for Elements might be more than you'll want to invest. Adobe's user interface philosophy does not vibrate particularly well with me, yet I have become quite comfortable working with Premiere Elements.

Ulead and Pinnacle Systems both offer video creation tools, however the latter company was unwilling to send us a press evaluation copy and its web site does not offer a free trial. That typically suggests a red flag for us in the customer service area, but your mileage might vary. Ulead's MediaStudio Pro is an impressive $399 bundle with many intuitive and friendly features for capturing video, integrating audio, and assembling the pieces of a slide show. It includes the highly-regarded SmartSound technology for customized creation of royalty-free audio to fit any length of video. Its output options are limited, however, and DVD creation requires a separate application.

Which brings us to Pro Show from Photodex, the most intuitive and "creative-friendly" application we know of for digital photographers.

You can start with a free trial download of the $20 Pro Show and within less than 10 minutes (seven to be exact, but who's counting...other than us), be creating slide shows from your photos. You'll want to get to at least the $45 Pro Show Gold level to enjoy captioning, transparency, better motion control, and DVD creation. The $250 Producer version supports RAW photo formats, hyperlinked captions, DVD menu creation, and perhaps most important, support for multiple layers on a slide, making picture-in-picture and similar effects routine.

Pro Show will import all forms of video but it does not capture video. If your work is primarily video capture and editing, you'd be better off with Elements, or offerings from Ulead or Pinnacle. But if most of your work is with photos, Pro Show offers unparalleled flexibility (and with Microsoft Movie Maker available for free to all

Please Insert Program Diskette

Before I criticize Photodex for its draconian policies, I will laud its developers for a clever form of copy protection by way of a hardware key—a small USB device that must be plugged into a port in order for the program to run. There are no restrictions on how many times you install the software and on how many machines, but it can only be operating at the location that houses the hardware key.

This is as ingenuous as it is troubling. Photodex cuts you little slack if you lose it, charging a hefty replacement fee. And there are just enough reports of hardware keys not being recognized by the program to call into question this strategy.

But these factors are not what bother us about the hardware key; we fear the specter of the idea catching on. What if other programs begin instituting the hardware key? What if a half dozen of your primary apps all require them? You would need to invest in a USB hub just for the keys.

Ultimately, this could send us back to the 1980s, when you needed a "program diskette" in order to run Lotus 1-2-3, dBase, and WordPerfect. If this idea takes hold, we would have to carry around multiple hardware keys to run our software, amounting to a colossal step backward in software portability. This is why we hope that Photodex and all other software makers choose to forego or never pursue hardware-based copy protection.

Windows users, you can always use it to capture video and save it to a format that Pro Show can import).

Pro Show's interface invites experimentation on the path to learning. If you're not sure what you can do with a photo that you have dragged to your timeline, just double-click it and a window full of all controls and effects appears. Double-click an audio clip and you will be taken directly to all soundtrack options. Adding a transition between slides is as simple as clicking between the two slides. No other program provides this level of control in such an intuitive way.

Finally, Pro Show Gold's and Producer's output choices are positively dizzying. You can export your slide shows as MPEG-1 or -2 video, compressed and uncompressed AVI, high-resolution executable file for Windows PCs, a web stream, five flavors of video CD, low-res emailable version, and DVD, either direct burn or ISO creation. The newest version also offers an export directly to Flash and QuickTime format, addressing long-standing deficiencies in Mac support.

Making Memories, Evoking Emotions

Why has this chapter turned its focus toward Pro Show? Because it is without peer in the niche with which PowerPoint users find frustration: professional-grade synchronization of photography with audio. Nothing stirs the senses like still imagery set to music, but PowerPoint is just not up to snuff.

Pro Show Producer is. It enjoys that almost-magical quality of making sense the moment you begin working with it. This was so pronounced for me that I almost literally established a new business as a result of our ability to connect with the software, and if you visit the Portfolio page at www.PhotosToMemories.net, you will see examples of photo slide shows that were created and published in just days.

Coupled with the $99 Premiere Elements and various free applications, all of your bases are covered. This partnership of software can take you leagues beyond PowerPoint's Photo Album feature.

Here are the basics for creating a project that blends video, photos, and music. We're keeping it general anticipating that most of you don't own the software and perhaps have never even heard of it.

Step One: Create a Project Folder

Because advanced video creation software uses media by reference (instead of trying to import it), it is essential that you organize your work diligently. This isn't hard to do, just easily overlooked. On our

Figure 20.1

Many different file formats are involved in video projects so good organization is key.

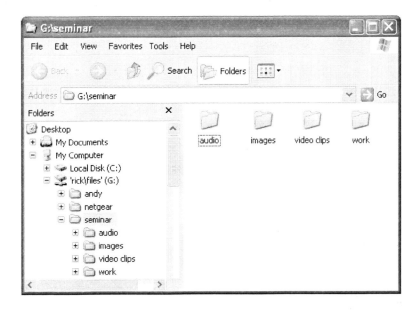

system, Drive G is where we create our videos, and for a project like a promo for a seminar, we recommend the simple folder structure shown in Figure 20.1: a folder for audio clips, one for video footage, one for photos and other still images, and one for any handiwork needed in an image-editing or drawing program (i.e., if you needed to create a complex transparency in Photoshop or a powerclip in CorelDraw, the result would go in the images folder, but the native application file would be stored in the work folder).

Step Two: Create Video Footage First

Motion video requires more pre-production work than still photos so our best advice is to take care of it first if your project has any. Again, we have found the $99 Premiere Elements a handy one-stop shop for capturing video from Firewire or USB sources, trimming and editing, adding transitions, and tweaking audio.

Export all video clips as uncompressed AVI files—720 x 480 resolution (if in North America or another NTSC country; 720 x 576 if in a country that uses the PAL standard), 29.97 frames per second, full RGB color palette, and audio set at 16-bit, 48,000 Hz (CD quality). These settings imply two things:

■ You will have tremendous flexibility to use this video. You can place it in high-fidelity projects or downsample it for delivery across the web.

▓ It will take up gobs of hard drive space, about 100MB for 30 seconds of video. If your work involves motion video, get used to the fact that you will need a much larger hard drive.

It is likely that the video you capture with Premiere will be in AVI format, and if you follow our recommendation, you will be exporting your final clips in AVI format. This can be confusing and Premiere doesn't help with a seemingly random automatic naming scheme for captured video. Therefore, you will want a naming scheme that enables you to keep this all straight, and possibly a folder in addition to video clips: raw or captured footage.

Step Three: Gather Photos

Your movie might have two or three video clips, but it could have hundreds of photos, and keeping them all straight can be a chore. If your movie has definable sections, give each one a letter and then number the photos within those lettered sections. Before long, you'll be able to see the structure of your movie through your photos.

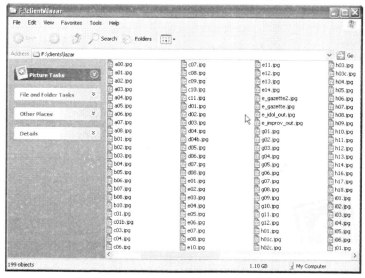

Step Four: Choose Audio

Sometimes this decision is not yours to make; other times, the photos themselves suggest musical themes. In either case, you'll want to begin gathering candidates—the more the better. If you're gathering music through your iTunes account, see the upcoming sidebar "It's Your Music!"

Step Five: Begin Assembly

Let the creativity begin! Here is where you assemble all of the pieces, creating meaningful imagery, evocative integration of sound and music, and elegant transitions between passages. If you like working with music and pictures, you will find few computer projects more satisfying than this one.

Walking Through a Video Project

I was recently hired by three siblings to create a tribute for their parents who were about to celebrate 50 years of marriage. Three generations of the Lazar family were meeting at a Club Med to celebrate and they wanted to play the movie for the couple there. I didn't know this family before they hired me, would only meet two of the siblings, had never met the anniversary couple, and would not meet them throughout the process. Ditto for the many grandkids whose images I would be showcasing. This proved to be a challenge, as expected: how to develop familiarity—intimacy, really—with people whom I didn't know.

The first step was to gather photos...lots and lots of photos. Most of their archives were prints, which meant no small amount of scanning. Some of the photos were in 35mm slide format, requiring a trip to a scanning service.

Once the scanning was done, we needed to identify the players, and ACDSee proved helpful for this task with its Print Contact Sheet command. We could survey over 100 photos in seven sheets of laser-printed paper.

This process involved two of the siblings, Mark and Suzanne, reminiscing over just about every photo and sharing stories that put the images in context. They tried to make it seem as if this were for my benefit, but it was clear they were cherishing the opportunity to look back. I kept thinking to myself, "If they're getting misty over little black-and-white thumbnails, imagine how they're going to respond if I do my job right..."

We identified numerous sections, gave them all names (Intro, Courtship, Weddings, Vacations, Grandkids, Finale), and assigned each section a number, as described above.

The Lazars had a few songs that carried special family meaning—a Tijuana Brass song from the 1970s and a crazy version of Cocktails for Two with hilarious sound effects—and otherwise looked to me for suggestions. I went with one cliché (the 1970s Sister Sledge hit,

It's Your Music!

Overcoming the oppressive restrictions of iTunes

I had swallowed my frustration for months. I was only paying 99 cents per song, so on what grounds did I have to complain too much? Still, the notion that a song I buy from iTunes can only be played within iTunes or on an iPod seemed like a policy created by IBM, not Apple.

My frustration bubbled over due to the experiences of a family member not those of my own. My sister Jody, who has had nothing but trouble with her iPod, shared with me the public venting of a New York Times journalist (www.altman.com/editorial/archive/06apr01.htm).

While I do not own an iPod, I buy my share of songs from iTunes, and I find it to be the height of arrogance that a song I rightfully own cannot travel with me outside of something beginning with a lower-case i. When it began to impede on my digital video business, I knew I needed to find a solution.

So I went back to my childhood. I used to spend untold hours recording music to cassette. First it was AM top-40 music, then the higher-fidelity FM stations, and ultimately my records. I would lose a bit of fidelity from the vinyl, but it was worth it to be able to play music from my records anywhere I wanted. Funny how far we've come and yet what a giant step backwards we've taken.

"We Are Family"), a personal favorite ("These are Days" from 10,000 Maniacs), an old reliable (The Jimmy Cliff version of "I Can See Clearly Now"), and a classic (John Lennon's "In My Life" from the Beatles' Rubber Soul album).

Using commercial music for personal projects that you do not distribute is fine. If you try to publicly distribute it or charge for it to be viewed, you must seek permission from the publisher.

I was now ready to turn to Pro Show Producer and begin taking these raw materials and turning them into something that this family could keep and cherish for decades. That sounds sappy, I know, but it really happens. You can't imagine until you get a chance to do it the feeling

And then I encountered an alarmingly simple shareware program called Any Sound Recorder. It is one of several programs that does exactly what its name implies: it digitally records any sound that emanates from your sound card. It has become my answer to Apple.

When I buy a song from iTunes, the first thing I do now is record it to CD-quality WAV format, replace the purchased file with the WAV file, and say goodbye to all restrictions. As far as iTunes is concerned, the WAV file is a piece of music that is entirely outside of its jurisdiction. While the song will play in iTunes, burn to a CD, and transfer to an iPod, iTunes does not nag me about authorization or give me any grief should I ever want to convert it to another format.

The WAV file is much larger than the purchased file, but that is my prerogative: I could have chosen to save it as MP3 or in one of several more compressed (and lower fidelity) flavors. If I wanted to cart thousands of songs on a portable player, I would choose to do that, but I have hundreds, not thousands, I have a large hard drive in my PC, and I love the notion of having a high-quality original audio file, from which I could create compressed versions at will.

At $24.95, this program is a trivial expense. The more significant outlay is your time: Any Sound Recorder (ASR) and programs like it do not "convert" your songs; they record them. Therefore, after you have paid your .99 to buy a five-minute song, you will need to

continued...

derived from creating something that has such an impact on an entire family. And I actually get paid to do it...

Basic Mechanics

Pro Show Producer offers a Timeline view, but most who use it prefer the so-called Slide List view, where the order of photos and videos is represented by thumbnails, without regard for how long each one is displayed. Audio tracks are shown below the slides and duration and transition are easily discerned as well.

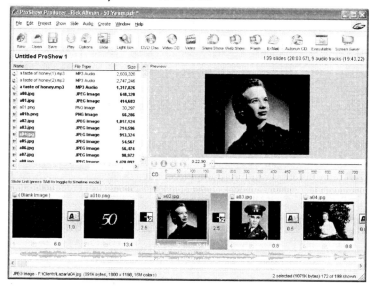

Double-clicking a slide invokes a dialog box with every command, effect, setting, or function available within the application. While this probably looks daunting at first, there is tremendous comfort in

...continued from previous page

spend five minutes playing it while ASR is listening. If you have a library of thousands, you would probably choose to do this on an as-needed basis.

ASR is as good as your sound card, but if your sound card were a piece of junk, you would already know it because your purchased music would sound terrible. And while there might be some measurable drop in fidelity running the music through your PC's circuitry, when compared to what I used to do with my cassette deck, the compromise is so small as to be laughable.

This is all completely legal. You own the music and provided you do not intend to resell it or distribute it illegally, you are perfectly entitled to manipulate it to suit your needs. (My republishing of

knowing that you won't have to wade through the entire interface to look for a particular effect. You'll have to wade through this dialog box, but that's not as arduous.

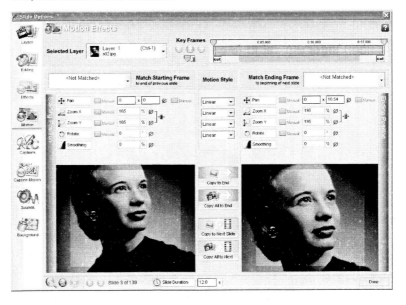

You can see by the before and after images or by the change in Pan and Zoom values that the effect we have applied to the above photo is a vertical pan and simultaneous gradual zoom in, across a duration of 12 seconds. Once comfortable with the software, this would take you about 10-15 seconds to perform. Imagine how long it would take to do this in PowerPoint, where you would have to add two separate animations and then time them both out for 12 seconds (which is not one of the pre-set durations).

the NYT article at my web site is probably more of a violation than anything discussed here.)

You can also record Internet radio with ASR. I listen to an iTunes stream and as a song is about to begin, I tap a key to launch a script that activates ASR's record command. If I don't like the song, I stop the recording. If I do like it, I wait for it to end, trim off any fat at the beginning or end, save it as a WAV file, and drag it into iTunes. These recordings are typically not of the same quality as purchased music (depending on the quality of the stream), but they'll do.

Any Sound Recorder fills the bill very nicely for me and solves a problem that Apple deserves shame for creating.

If you double-click the soundtrack, you'll get a set of controls for handling fades in and out, start and length of the clip, and what to do with the soundtrack during slides that have their own audio. I love being able to gradually fade the music if a slide includes a narration or other type of audio.

That's pretty much all you need to know to begin to create a video montage and set it to music. The rest comes from your own imagination and sense of the occasion.

Looking for Visual Themes
While each section of this video is distinct, I tried to create a visual thread that could run throughout. I chose a current photo of the couple and used PhotoPaint's SketchPad effect to create an abstract image.

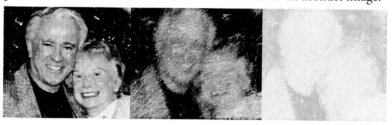

I then placed that in the background of any slide that didn't contain a full-slide photo. All section beginnings and endings would show this abstract image. For example, the slide below shows a composite of three separate photos of the siblings when they were young, with that abstract photo behind them. Then the siblings gradually fade away, leaving only the background.

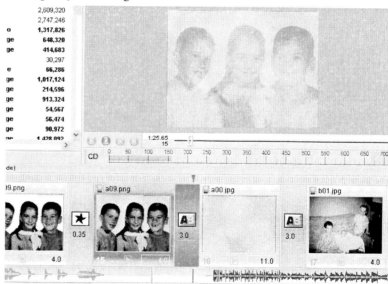

Another section placed photos inside feathered vignettes, with the abstract image as their background.

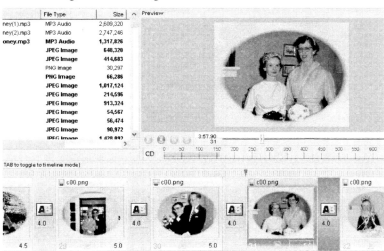

Integration

We integrated two video segments—one of three grandkids singing a song and one of the great-grandfather telling jokes, as he was want to do during family gatherings. We thought it would be fun to create a fake newsletter, have it spin in (like they used to do in the "Extra! Extra!" days), and then have the video play in the space of the newsletter photo, as is happening on Slide 57.

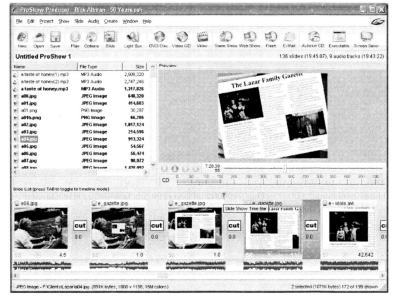

We also made use of many semi-transparent photos to create a dreamy quality during appropriate passages. Beatles fans will recognize George Martin's short but beautiful piano solo during In My Life as an opportune time to create that type of mood.

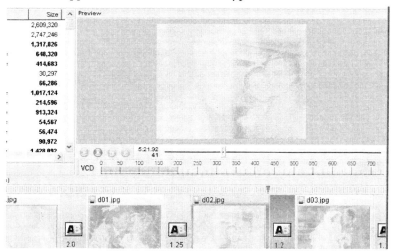

If after watching this video, you do not like the synchronization of audio and imagery, blame me, not the software. Pro Show Producer is accurate to fractions of a second, providing the author with total control of the mix. In the intro, I bring childhood photos of the three siblings in over photos of their parents, each one right on the toot of a French horn. Once I time it out, it will be accurate every single time. PowerPoint does not cache audio and photo information the same way, so every time you play a slide show, it will be a bit different. In short, I would not even attempt a tight sync like that in PowerPoint.

At the very end of the video—as Natalie Cole crooned "You must remember this, a kiss is but a kiss..."—I allowed the abstract photo to gradually blend into the actual photo, with an overlay of "50 Years of Love and Family."

That final text overlay turned out to be the only text in the entire video. That was a choice made by the three siblings, a good choice in my view. If this video were for a wider audience, it would have been prudent to identify the people and the scenes more often. But the 17 people who would be at the celebration and then be viewing it from their DVD players later would need no assistance with the people and events being shown.

As a keepsake video to be shown decades from now, you could make the argument that the people should be identified, but that's the beauty of digital video: the Lazars can always revisit it to make those types of changes.

Mission Accomplished

The entire video is just under 20 minutes, which is longer than I normally recommend if a large audience were watching it. But a gathering of family and close friends could probably watch an hour of this stuff, so I never advise that my clients shorten a video if there is a lot of meaningful material.

Start to finish was a month, but that included many days at a time waiting to receive scans and sending proofs and waiting to receive feedback. Once the photos, video, and music were chosen, the bulk of the work came together in about five days, and the many tweaks and refinements consumed another five days. Then I took almost one entire day to design the artwork for the DVD itself and burn and print seven copies.

▼ Download and view this video at betterppt.com/ lazar.htm

I have really come to appreciate my Epson Stylus Photo printer that has a special adapter that feeds a DVD or CD as if it were paper and prints directly onto it. If this type of work interests you, you should download the video just to see the software's prowess with output. We have made two choices available to you:

- For Windows users, an executable (.exe) file that requires nothing else in order to run. It is a 52MB file that runs in an 800x600 window and features full-fidelity audio. For a 19-minute video, that is incredibly compact.

- For any web surfer, a Flash file that needs only a standard browser plug-in to play. Fades are slightly grainy, but otherwise, image quality and audio fidelity are excellent. The Flash video weighs in at 80MB but as a stream, begins playing almost immediately after the download begins.

There are plenty of other output formats—I can even create a version of this that plays on your smartphone and video iPod.

▼ Scary stat of the day: All of the artwork for this book consumes under 400MB of file space. The video components of just this chapter require over 5GB.

Part Four: Working Smarter

Our Toolbox

In addition to the two main programs described here, I regularly call upon the following applications when creating movies:

CorelDraw Graphics Suite

For a fraction of the price of Adobe Photoshop, you get an excellent image-editing program and a best-of-breed vector drawing program. The perfect creative suite for digital movie makers. www.corel.com

SnagIt

No self-respecting software trainer can get by without the ability to capture screen images or create video of a program being driven, and Snag-It from TechSmith is our choice. www.techsmith.com

Kinoma Producer

To create videos in unusual formats, like for an iPod or a Palm, you need an intelligent video encoder. This handy suite from Kinoma does just that, and for a very friendly price of just $30. Output on our Treo 650 is remarkably sharp, good enough for us to use to show videos to prospective clients without having to schlep our notebook PC around. www.kinoma.com

WavePad

An excellent wave file editor, and completely free. www.nch.com.au/wavepad

Any Sound Recorder

See my sidebar rant about songs copy-protected by iTunes... www.any-sound-recorder.com

Audacity

Another good and free sound editor that will also record music from iTunes and other sources. http://audacity.sourceforge.net.

Chapter 21

Junk & Miscellany

Even across 21 chapters, I seem to be unable to write a book in which all the topics I wish to cover fall neatly into categories. Good thing, too—these potpourri chapters are usually the most popular. I always save them for the end and add to the list of topics as I write the book. And now, as I sit poised to compile this final chapter, I wonder if I shouldn't just wait and save it for an entirely new book. I can see it now on the shelves: *PowerPoint Junk and Miscellany*, by John Doe. (Would you put your name on that book title?)

Without further ado, here is a loosely organized collection of thoughts, advice, commentary, tips and tricks, and miscellaneous junk about PowerPoint.

Version 2007

I approach this first topic with no small amount of uncertainty and reluctance. There is a lot to like in PowerPoint 2007 and it is easier to make a legitimately attractive slide deck with it than with any previous version. But if I'm being completely honest, I would have to admit that I have no plans to switch to it exclusively.

I love what Microsoft has done with slide mastering, and the new graphics engine is terrific. On more than one occasion, I have started a project in 2007 to take advantage of the new features, and then saved it down to 2003 and continued the work to completion.

Presentation files degrade quite gracefully, too. Figures 21.1–21.3 show two new features completely foreign to earlier versions

Figure 21.1
These photos were controlled by a slide master in 2007 and are now just slide elements when converted down and opened in version 2003.

Figure 21.2
PowerPoint 2007 converts special layouts on slide masters to standard placeholders in earlier versions.

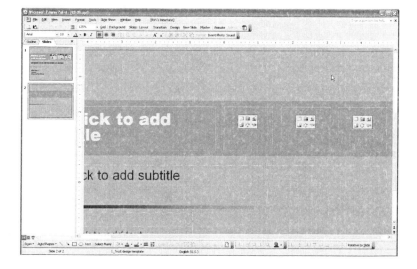

nonetheless performing quite well in version 2003. Figure 21.1 and 2 show the special title slide layout that I created back in Chapter 8 (page 60), with the photos that I place on one title, and a blank title slide awaiting my input. The intelligence that we built into the slide master in 2007 was removed, but they were converted down to something that makes sense (placeholders on the slide itself).

Figure 21.3
Photo effects in 2007 convert down to transparent graphics.

Meanwhile the photo manipulations in Figure 21.3 are no longer dynamic, but they look every bit as good.

As impressive as the backward compatibility is, why do I resort to it? Because my ability to crank out slides in 2007 is severely impaired by the Ribbon and by the inflexibility of the interface. To be fair, the Ribbon is no worse than the old paradigm of a Menu bar...unless you are accustomed to moving quickly with a combination of mouse clicks and keystrokes. Then you would be utterly frustrated if you, say, had two objects selected and you wanted to bottom align them. In 2007, that maneuver requires three clicks and a trip almost all the way across the screen.

I respect Microsoft's desire to cater to new and occasional users, and to be sure, the Ribbon is better than a factory-configured Menu bar that hides over 70% of its commands. In moving in this direction, however, without providing provision for advanced users to create access to commands to which they have grown accustomed—that is insulting.

I did discover that if you close your eyes and type the keystrokes you know by heart from earlier versions (Alt+F | A for Save As, Alt+D | S for Slide Show Setup), 2007 will actually launch the command. And

Part Four: Working Smarter

as I noted in Chapter 17, there are third-party utilities on the verge of being released that might address the plight of the advanced user.

But we shouldn't have to resort to blind keystrokes or third-party add-ins, and that suggests that Microsoft is ignoring an entire sect of its user base. Of course, we only have to return to Chapter 1 to understand the company's logic: it wants to go after the 15-minute set—the ones who only learned the first 15 minutes worth of the software.

I have come to embrace the new features; I have come to loathe the new interface.

Never Paste Again!

Do you actually know what goes on when you use the Clipboard to transfer text or a graphic from another application? Do you know what you are really asking for when you press Ctrl+V or click the Paste icon?

Most don't. If they did, they might never do it again.

The Windows Clipboard is a more sophisticated tool than most know, able to carry many formats of an element at once. In fact, when you copy something to the Clipboard, you are usually placing the object there in many different formats. Furthermore, the default choice—the one you get when you ask for Paste—is often problematic:

- With a graphic, the default choice is an OLE-linked graphic that will attempt to open the native application if you double-click the graphic. If you share this with others, who do not own that application, fireworks could result.

- With text from a word processor, it is HTML-formatted rich text in the size and typeface of the original. If you are pasting text into a list of bullets, that's the last thing you want.

Sometimes the default choice is correct. And sometimes PowerPoint provides a safety net via its Smart Paste feature, if turned on in Options. But we don't want you playing roulette with your slides. We want you to make informed choices when you transfer information into PowerPoint.

We want you to use Paste Special.

The Paste Special dialog box shows all of the flavors available to you, enabling you to choose the right one. It's not always obvious which is

the right one, but with experience you'll get better. In the case of a
CorelDraw graphic

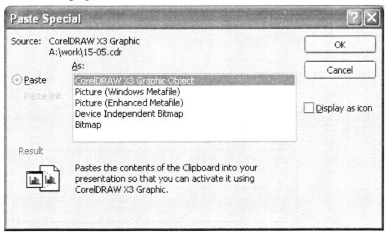

the default choice embeds the entire graphic, editable from a double-
click. This sounds attractive, but since OLE was first introduced in
1992, it has never lived up to its promise, remaining fraught with sta-
bility problems.

If the graphic you created is made up of vector objects, you would
want to choose the Windows Metafile format; if the graphic is mostly
bitmap data, you would want to choose Device Independent Bitmap.

In the case of text, if you are pasting lines of text into a series of bullets, you would most likely want the text to conform to the format
you have established for those bullets. That means choosing Unfor-
matted Text from Paste Special.

If you are copying and pasting within the same application, then you
can just use the straight Paste command. Otherwise, you act the most
prudently and responsibly when you survey your choices first.

On my customized interface, I have removed the Paste icon from the
Standard toolbar and replaced it with Paste Special.

Heading Out the Door

Here are the first of two gigantic topics that we have largely ignored
in the first 20 chapters. Most of this book assumes that you are creating a presentation that lives on your notebook and will be delivered
from your notebook...by you. Indeed, distributing a presentation
remains a mystery to many. I have a colleague who wants to write an
entire book on this subject; imagine how he will feel when he realizes

that I'm stuffing the subject into a junk chapter at the end of the book. Oh well, one less free copy I have to send out...

How wide an audience?

The first question to address will go a long way toward helping you devise a strategy: The people to whom you are distributing your presentation—do they own PowerPoint?

- Are they colleagues at your workplace, where you can safely assume they own Office?

- Or is this going on a web site or some other point of mass distribution, where anyone might download it?

If you can answer Yes to the first question, your life just got easier: you distribute a PowerPoint file. You still have questions to address, but at least you know what it is you are sending out. If your presentation requires the use of exits, motion paths, or simultaneous animations, you will need to consider the likelihood that a PowerPoint 2000 user might try to view it. And if your presentation requires specific typefaces, you'll need to find out if you are allowed to embed them with the presentation.

The simpler you can make your presentation, the greater chance of distribution success you stand. To wit:

- Can you just use Arial? If so, do.

- Can the slides just advance, without the need for fancy animation? If so, let them.

- Can you do without macros? If so, do without.

Now your PowerPoint universe is about as wide as it can be.

No PowerPoint? No problem...

If you cannot count on your audience owning PowerPoint, the situation is a bit more complicated, and again there are two questions to address:

- Do you send your presentation in a different format?

- Do you try to give them PowerPoint?

If you determine that you can live without PowerPoint, there are three almost-universal formats that could help you. The place to start is HTML, because every computer built since 1996 knows what to do when you double-click an .htm file. And if you have never saved your presentation to HTML, you might be surprised at how much is

Figure 21.5
Browsers are better than you might think at preserving the look and feel of a PowerPoint presentation..

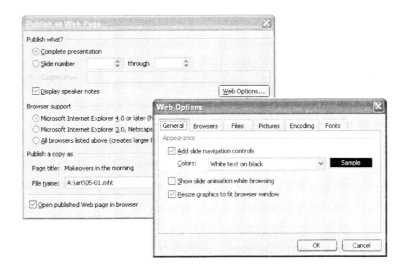

preserved. Typefaces, animations, and transitions can all be maintained to some degree, and Figure 21.5 shows some of the controls available to you.

A second possibility is Adobe Acrobat. While you can't create a PDF file directly from a PowerPoint command (unless you use version 2007 and have installed the free add-in), you can go the conventional route of printing to the Acrobat print driver. Once done, use Acrobat's Document Properties to ask for the file to be opened full-screen, and Edit Preferences | Full Screen to choose a default transition and an auto-advance interval.

If your colleagues can't open a PDF file, you work in a very obscure industry. Even my father—the 87-year-old semi-retired rocket scientist who still uses Lotus 1-2-3 for his propulsion formulas—can open a PDF file.

And a third is Flash, the rich format of the Web. If you're just showing slides, go with HTML or Acrobat. But if you need a more robust offering of your ideas—audio, mood-evoking transitions, careful sequencing of images or text—Flash would answer the call for you, and there are numerous companies taking up the challenge of accurate conversion from PowerPoint to Flash.

It would not be completely objective for me to proclaim that PointeCast (www.pointecast.com) leads the charge on this front, seeing how the company has been a PowerPoint Live sponsor for the past three years. But PointeCast Publisher has garnered much praise among end-users with whom we regularly communicate. WildPresenter Pro (www.wildform.com) is also well-regarded for its conversion tools, as is TechSmith's Camtasia (www.techsmith.com).

Part Four: Working Smarter

Through it all, though, the best way to faithfully represent a Power-Point file is with PowerPoint itself. Microsoft freely distributes its so-called Viewer for those who want to send a PowerPoint file without regard for whether the recipient owns the software.

The gateway for using the Viewer is the poorly-named Package for CD function (most people who use it regularly use it to copy a presentation to another folder, not to a CD). It gathers up all of the components of a presentation—linked audio clips or movies, embedded fonts, and any other file you designate—and copies them to a location of your choosing, along with the Viewer files.

Name	Size	Type	Date Modified
pptview.exe	1,638 KB	Application	7/7/2005 3:57 PM
gdiplus.dll	1,732 KB	Application Extension	7/5/2005 12:05 PM
intldate.dll	64 KB	Application Extension	3/17/2005 1:43 PM
ppvwintl.dll	126 KB	Application Extension	3/17/2005 1:07 PM
saext.dll	207 KB	Application Extension	7/14/2003 10:57 PM
unicows.dll	241 KB	Application Extension	10/30/2002 12:21 PM
pvreadme.htm	5 KB	HTML Document	7/25/2003 12:32 PM
09-03.ppt	892 KB	Microsoft Office Po...	2/27/2007 7:06 PM
play.bat	1 KB	MS-DOS Batch File	2/27/2007 7:06 PM
AUTORUN.INF	1 KB	Setup Information	2/27/2007 7:06 PM
playlist.txt	1 KB	Text Document	2/27/2007 7:06 PM
sound02.wav	100 KB	Wave Sound	12/20/2005 9:08 PM

This group of files all needs to be transported at once to the recipient's computer, and that presents challenges of its own. A presentation with external elements cannot be shown from a remote URL; PowerPoint won't find an MP3 or AVI file out on a web page.

The entire group of files must make its way onto a drive that has a letter or a network path, and we have a detailed recommendation about how to perform this at www.altman.com/editorial/archive/05mar.htm.

Creating Self-Running Presentations

Here's the second big topic that we have largely ignored: how do you create a PowerPoint file for a presentation that you are not there to deliver? A unique set of demands prevails over the PowerPoint file that is unaccompanied by a presenter. In fact, many of the proclamations that we have made across the first 21 chapters need to be softened a bit when we talk about PowerPoint files that must present themselves. To wit:

Don't try so hard

We've whined and complained about presentations that bid for our attention with loud and unprofessional tactics. Chapter 3 is entitled "Look at Me!" and rails against excessive efforts by slide creators to have their slides noticed.

But let's face it, the humanless presentation *does* have to try harder. In the absence of a human voice, slides do need to pump up the volume a bit to create energy.

Don't be so obnoxious

In Chapter 5, we bemoan "the scourge that is custom animation," and are merciless with those who employ gratuitous animation.

But a self-running presentation has lots of competition. Your viewers are likely to be doing other things at the same time—working email, making phone calls, hanging out at iTunes. They might not even be looking at the screen, and so you would need to be overt to get their attention, taking advantage of Universal Axiom No. 3 (if stuff moves, you have to look).

Just use Wipe and Fade

If one of your viewers is distracted, you'll need a transition that is more invasive. You'll need something that (gasp) moves across the screen. A boomerang is still not necessary, but a slide transition that pushes the ending slide out and the new slide in might be just right.

No Hidden Hyperlinks

To insure against your viewers getting lost or just losing interest, you'll need immaculate and obvious navigation. They will need to see a menu that makes total sense and makes them feel that they can always access it. They advance slides, you don't, and they need to know how and when to do it. If you create web sites, your navigation skills will become valuable.

◆

One of the reasons that we buried this topic here is because we don't have any good data on how many of our readers create self-running presentations. Please let us know if this topic is vital to your work with presentations and we'll promote it to a chapter. Send us email at betterppt@altman.com. That will also give us a good idea of how many readers actually made it all the way back here to the nether regions of Chapter 21.

Now, time for more junk...

Start Me Up...

I expect that most of you know that F5 starts a presentation. If you didn't know that, now you do: pressing F5 from anywhere while in Edit mode automatically switches you into Slide Show mode (i.e. your presentation will run). That beats the heck out of mousing up to the View menu or Ribbon and then clicking Slide Show.

In Version 2003, PowerPoint inherited an even better keystroke: Shift+F5. When you're building a presentation, you probably spend a great deal of time checking out how particular slides look and perform; if you're working on Slide 70, you're not terribly interested in starting your slide show from the beginning, and you might have grown to loathe that tiny icon in the lower-left corner called Slide Show from Current Slide. Loathe no more—just press Shift+F5, and you will be whisked into Slide Show mode starting at whatever slide you're on.

But not too many of you knows what happens if you press and hold Ctrl while clicking that tiny Show from Current Slide icon. Do you know? The slide show plays in a small window at the top-left corner of your screen:

When I first discovered this, I immediately wondered why I couldn't press Ctrl+Shift+F5 to make this happen, but that's because I'm never satisfied and I always search the mouths of gift horses. Still, it's a way-cool trick for times when you want to see how a slide behaves and be able to work on that slide at the same time (changes made in Edit mode are dynamic and immediately show up in the Slide Show window.

So that got me thinking...maybe there are other buried treasures around this part of the interface...so I started poking around...and this is what I found...

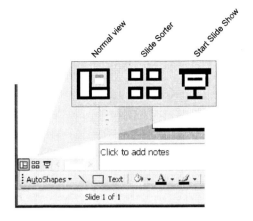

Keystroke	Icon	Result
Shift	Normal View	Enter Slide Master view
Shift	Slide Sorter	Enter Handout Master view
Shift	Start Slide Show	Set Up Show dialog
Ctrl	Start Slide Show	Run slide show in small window
Alt	Start Slide Show	Run slide show in Browse mode*

* Browse by Individual mode: Slide Show | Setup Show | Show Type | Browsed by An Individual

Also, don't forget that there are Play and Slide Show icons in the Animation task pane. The Play button plays the current slide right on the slide, to help you with timing and sequencing, and the Slide Show button is the same as the tiny one at the lower-left (but bigger and easier to click on!).

It's Midnight—Do You Know Where Your Templates Are?

Back in Chapter 8, we all but mocked PowerPoint's template structure, pointing out that any presentation can act like a template and any PowerPoint file can be turned into a template by changing its extension to .pot. (And no, we did not wonder out loud what they were smoking up in Redmond when they chose that extension...we decided to hold that for our junkie chapter, I mean our junk chapter.)

All fine and well...but where should a template reside in order to show up in PowerPoint's Design task pane? That's not so obvious, for three reasons: 1) The Documents and Settings folder can be treacherous to navigate; 2) The folder that you need to find is hidden by Windows; and 3) You can do everything right and still not see your template.

If you want to convert one of your own PowerPoint files into a template, so it can be used from within the application, your course of action should be easy:

1. Open the file.

2. Go to File | Save As and change the file type to Design Template

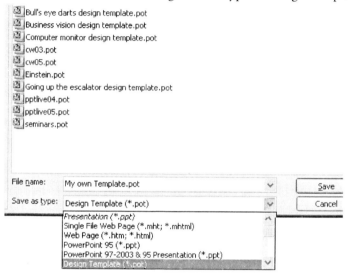

PowerPoint will automatically change the file window to the special Templates folder.

That should be all there is to it...but it's not. In what could only be described as a bug in the program, your new template will not show up in the Design task pane's thumbnails of templates until it is actually used once. (Kind of like needing to have already gotten a loan in order to be granted your first loan.) So the first time you want to use this template, you must click the Browse button at the bottom of the task pane and go find it. Once done, its thumbnail will take up permanent residence in the task pane.

What if you receive a template file from a colleague? Would you know where to place it? As we mentioned earlier, navigating Documents and Settings is hard enough—once you get there, you should see the Application Data folder.

Overheard at the PPT Newsgroup

Diane from Bell South Internet Group asked this question:

I am using Power Point to make simple slide shows for children to advance with a mouse click, as they work independently at the computer. I am narrating each slide. I want the program to ignore inadvertent mouse clicks until the narration is complete, then advance the slide the next time the mouse is clicked (even though children may take varying amounts of time to click the mouse). I do not want to use action buttons, just a simple mouse click where the cursor could be anywhere on the screen.

I find that the children are clicking the mouse and advancing the slides before the narration for each slide is complete. I cannot find any way to keep them from doing this. I don't want to time each slide, because the narration on the slides may be of varying lengths—some with longer narration, some with shorter narration.

This intriguing question got three completely different solutions, each full of merit. First came Ellen Finkelstein, author of the *How To Do Everything in PowerPoint* series of books:

You can disallow clicking to advance slides by choosing (in Power-Point 2002/2003) Slide Show | Slide Transition. In the Slide Transition task pane, uncheck the On Mouse Click check box in the Advance Slide section.

Then set automatic timings for each slide according to the length of the narration. After timing each slide's narration, select each slide and use the same transition to set its timing in the Automatically After text box in the same location I just mentioned.

Next came David Marcovitz, a Microsoft PowerPoint MVP and author of Powerful PowerPoint for Educators:

Here is a simple way to do what you want. First, set the slide transition for your slides so that they do not advance on mouse click. Next, create a rectangle that covers the entire slide. Select the rectangle and choose Format | Autoshape to set the rectangle to 99% transparent.

Now, you need to set the animation order. If you have a sound icon, then you already have an animation effect for the sound, so

continued...

I said, you should see the Application Data folder...where is it??

That folder is hidden by default...isn't that grand? To fix this permanently, from any My Computer or Windows Explorer window, or Folder Options in Control Panel, do this:

1. Go to Tools | Folder Options | View.

2. Click Show Hidden Files and Folders.

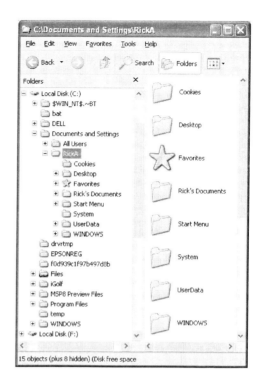

...continued from previous page
you need to make sure that the animation effect is set to With Previous.

Next, add an animation for your 99% transparent rectangle and set it to After Previous. To round out the animations, drag the sound's animation (in the custom animation task pane) above the rectangle's animation. Finally, you need to set a hyperlink or action setting for the 99% transparent rectangle to Next Slide.

What this will do is have the sound play and then bring in the rectangle (which the students won't actually see). While the sound is playing, the rectangle is not there, so a mouse click will not work. Once the sound has played and the rectangle has come in, any mouse click will have to be on the rectangle because it covers the whole slide, and the click will take you to the next slide.

Finally, John Wilson of the PowerPoint Alchemy web site (www.pptalchemy.co.uk) offered this:

In the slide transition pane, set the transition of the slide with narration to automatically after 0 seconds. Make the next slide a duplicate of this slide but with no narration. Set this slide to transition to On Click.

While you're here, uncheck Hide Extensions for Known File Types, because that is another completely brain-dead default. (What good comes of hiding extensions? Then you end up with file.pps.ppt when you are trying to create a PowerPoint file that runs when you double-click it.)

3. OK your way out.

Now you should see the Application Data folder and be able to navigate your way to the Templates subfolder.

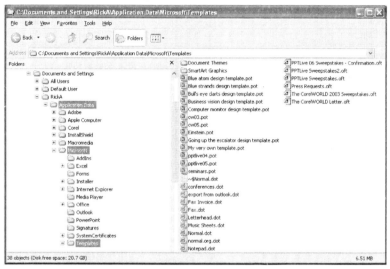

Notice that this folder is for all Office templates, not just PowerPoint ones. Copy any templates that you have acquired to this folder and then remember about needing a loan before getting your first one: click Browse to find that template file in the Design task pane. Then its thumbnail will show.

Disappearing Slide Masters

There is one more point of possible angst concerning templates: those with multiple sets of slide masters might be at risk of losing those masters that are not in use. In another example of creating trouble through simplification, PowerPoint will (sometimes) remove slide masters that are not in use.

To be precise, PowerPoint's slide masters (sometimes) default to not being "preserved"—that's the term that Microsoft uses for a slide master that should remain in the file even if it is not being used by any slides. This can be (sometimes) maddening and so you should be (sometimes) vigilant.

It's easy to be (sometimes) glib and (often) sarcastic in the last chapter of your book—why the *sometimes?* Because this doesn't always happen. About half the time, PowerPoint automatically preserves the masters. But when it doesn't, you're hosed. So get in the habit of always looking for the little push pin next to the slide master's thumbnail:

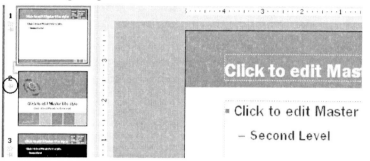

And if you don't see it, right-click the thumbnail and choose Preserve Master.

Bringing Object Order to Chaos

PowerPoint's object management is woeful. Objects are given unhelpful names (like Rectangle 23 or Shape 16) and there is no provision to rename them. PowerPoint 2007 finally addresses this; users of all earlier versions must purchase third-party tools or just build a bridge and get over it.

And that can be hard, even if you know about the hidden command called Select Multiple Objects, which shows you every object on a slide. In the case of a sequence of rectangles that needs to be animated in turn, you could drive yourself nuts trying to pick these out one after the other.

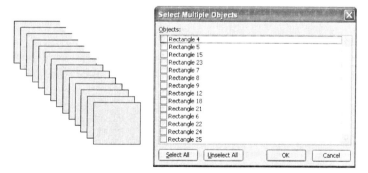

This is a typical situation, in which you did not create the rectangles in order or perhaps moved them around before putting them in sequence, so PowerPoint's names are completely confounding.

This requires a trip to the Format AutoShape dialog (available from the right-click or Format menu) and the seldom-used Web tab. If you create Alternative Text (as if you were going to create web links), that text shows up in the Select Multiple Objects dialog.

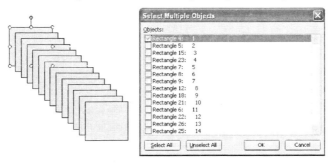

PowerPoint insists on using its own useless name for the object, but as you can see, even a simple Alternative Text entry such as a numeral can help. If you expect to have many overlapping objects, add a bit of Alternative Text (such as "This one goes on bottom!") and it can help you enormously when working through a formatting scheme.

Making Peace with Color Schemes

If I had the sense that PowerPoint users might wake up one day and become enamored and riveted by PowerPoint's engine for controlling color, this would become its own chapter.

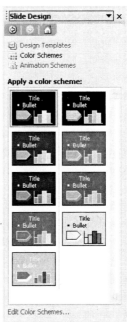

I have no such impression. Some very talented presentation designers completely ignore color schemes. But when we show how they are used at Power-Point Live, we turn heads right and left. So here is a brief tutorial on the function that you probably do not use but might wish that you did…

Every PowerPoint template (i.e., every PowerPoint file) has at least one color scheme and most have many.

Each of the schemes here are designed with eight complementary colors that generally look good together. Practicing with them is good for developing your eye, but its use can go well beyond that.

Figure 21.16
Think of a color scheme as a set of eight color definitions.

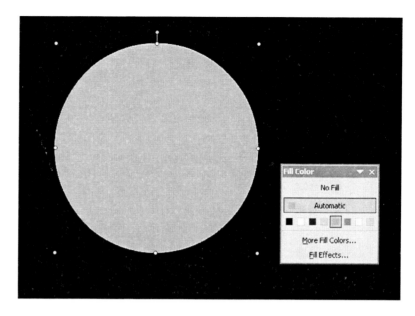

When you apply a color from the color scheme to an object on your slide, you are not just instructing the object to display a particular color. In the case of Figure 21.16, you are telling this circle, "you are to be filled with the color that is assigned to Position No. 5."

Position 5 happens to be a shade of blue right now, but it could be something different if you changed the definition for Position 5, used a different color scheme, or imported this slide into a different presentation.

If instead, you wanted to ensure that this circle is always a specific color, you would manually define that color, either with the standard or custom color palettes found if you choose More Fill Colors from the Fill Color dropdown or popup. Once you choose a manual color, it shows up on a line below the eight colors in the scheme, as shown in Figure 21.17.

You can now copy this circle to a different presentation file, move the whole slide there, swap in a different color scheme, or change out the entire template—this circle will remain the shade of blue that it is right now.

You can use this knowledge to great effect if you plan for it:

- If the Coca Cola Bottling Company hired you to create slides, you surely would not make Coca Cola Red one of the colors of the color scheme, where a different presentation might change it to Coca Cola Blue. You would create a custom color, so it would never change.

■ If you have designed some nice accent lines between the title and subtitle, you would want their colors to match the rest of the slide and change if you changed the color scheme. For that, you would pick one of the eight.

Download color_schemes. ppt from the betterppt.com web site for a demonstration of how color schemes operate.

Colors from the scheme can be chosen any time there is a question of fill or outline. I regularly create a gradient fill using two complementary colors so that if the scheme changes, the gradient will still look good. There is plenty more to know about color schemes, but the distinction between the eight colors of the scheme and manually-assigned colors is the part that any user can put into use right away.

Version 2007 has vastly improved color scheme dialogs. Maybe as more people migrate to it there will be a wider understanding and use of color schemes.

Figure 21.17
This color assignment will always be the same color, no matter where this circle goes.

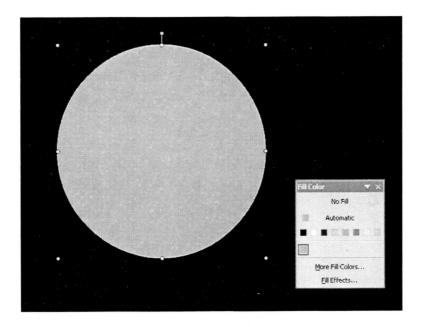

Dealing with Crappy Slides

What a great headline for the last topic of this book! We refer here to slides that are not necessarily poorly-designed (but probably), and not necessarily poorly-written (but probably), but the slide deck that has been *constructed* incorrectly. Bullets not in their placeholders... font assignments seven to a page...titles all different sizes...slides formatted one by one instead of through slide masters. That kind of crappy.

Part Four: Working Smarter

❶

❷

What exactly is curb appeal?

GOAL OF SESSION:

• To create an awareness and understanding of why it is important to maintain the aesthetic appeal and value of your homes.

• To give practical examples of how you can create that appeal.

• To inspire you to action.

❸

❹

• Makes the Community a "desired" place to live

• Safety Considerations

• Breaks downward cycle of deferred maintenance

• Creates emotional involvement by owners (engagement Vs. dial tone)

• *Creates a sense of neighborhood*

❺

❻

Before

After

❼

❽

Fences grow better when watered on a regular basis

The exercise yard at San Quentin???

And wow do we have a good example to use, as the slides on the preceding page point out. This presentation was delivered many times several years ago, and ironically, the presenter was so dynamic, he got good reviews despite the fact that his visuals were so bad.

If you were tasked with making this slide deck over, would you relish it or dread it? I was that person, and I did both. Here's a tour:

Slide 1

Quite possibly one of the worst title slides we have ever seen. This presentation was delivered to groups of homeowner associations and the idea of curb appeal was a good theme. But showing the opposite of curb appeal as the title? Not good...

Slide 2

Do we need a separate slide to ask this question? And if we do, must it have that papier mache background?

Slides 3 and 4

Here's the real pain. There were 33 slides just like these that were created using the Blank layouts and floating text placeholders. That means that I was unable to just reapply the slide layout to get rid of all of this hideous formatting. This would take some thought...

Slides 5 and 6

These were the first of 10 pairs of comparisons, but there was tremendous potential impact lost by not showing them on screen together. And we won't even talk about the smiley faces...

Slides 7 and 8

These are whimsical and warranted some form of cute treatment. But with the entire slide show feeling like a cartoon, these slides didn't seem to be different. Ironically, they needed to be cutesied up more.

The Makeover

I identified three basic types of slides—normal, before/after, and gotchas—and created slide masters for each. Nothing fancy; in fact just the opposite: these slides were crying out for a bit of conservatism. Blue backgrounds, white text for the regular slides, and black backgrounds for the before/afters and gotchas.

Just about anything would have been an improvement with the title slide. I was horrified to learn that it usually displayed for almost 10 minutes as audience members entered the ballroom. That's a long time for any static image, let alone a terrible one. Instead, I used the technique recommended at the end of Chapter 11 of fading a group of photos one atop the other.

The tricky part was creating the loop, so here's a challenge for you:

How do you make one slide loop indefinitely onto itself, and then when you are ready to begin your presentation, proceed to the second slide?

I'd love to hear from readers who have conjured up other solutions, but here is the one that I came up with:

1. Create two custom shows—one called Intro, containing just the first slide, and one called Main, containing every other slide in the deck, starting with the second one.

2. Go to Slide Show | Set Up Show and tell PowerPoint to run the Intro custom show. Also tell it to loop continuously.

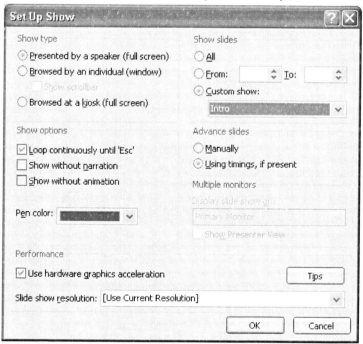

3. From the Transition task pane, choose a transition that fits with the action on the slide and set Advance Slide to Automatic After. For the After value, pick a duration that makes sense. For instance, my photo fades are six seconds apart, so I told the slide to wait for six seconds before "advancing," which would simply send it back to the beginning.

4. Draw a rectangle over the entire slide.

5. From Slide Show | Action Settings, set the click action to be a hyperlink to the custom show called Main.

6. Remove the fill and outline to make the rectangle invisible.

Now the first slide will loop until the presenter clicks on it once, at which point it will promptly advance to the second slide and then proceed from there.

As satisfying as this was to figure out, this challenge was nothing compared to the task of cleaning up the text. I only showed you two of those ill-crafted text slides back on page 262; there were actually over 30.

Let's take a moment to frame the problem. Having created a slide master for text slides, now I had to make all of the text slides conform to it. But none of the bullet slides was created using the standard text placeholders; the creator drew text boxes on blank slides and formatted them. As a result, reapplying the Title and Text layout would have no effect.

It would seem that my options were to retype the bullets into the proper placeholders (out of the question!) or try some cut-and-paste maneuver, which, even with a script to automate it, was unacceptable.

As with the loop, I'm not sure that there isn't a better way to solve this, and I hope to hear from others who have their own ideas. Here was mine, requiring an installed copy of Adobe Acrobat:

1. Print the entire presentation to a PDF file.

Part Four: Working Smarter

2. Open the PDF file in Adobe Acrobat and immediately perform a Save As to plain text. Call it anything, like makeover.txt.

3. Open makeover.txt in Notepad and find your titles and bullets. Enter tabs to identify bullets.

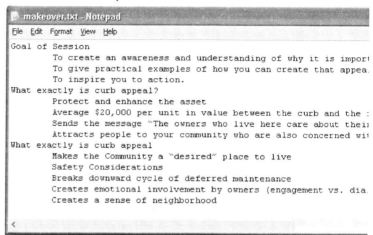

This presentation does not have any second-level bullets, but if it did, you would have entered a second tab for each of them.

4. Save and close the text file and return to PowerPoint.

5. Open the presentation file that has the redesigned slide masters and place your cursor where you want to insert the bullet slides.

6. Go to Insert | Slides From Outline and find makeover.txt. Voilà...

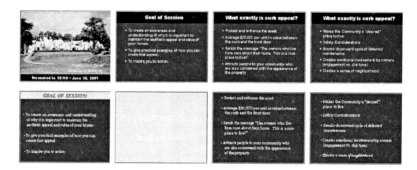

The top row of thumbnails are new slides; the bottom row are old ones. What I particularly like about this conversion technique is that it makes no distinction between types of text. Like the funky GOAL OF SESSION title that is stuffed into a filled rectangle (slide 5 above)—it all comes out as text, at which point I can delete unwanted text quickly and format bulleted text many, many times faster than I could cut and paste.

▼ Download before.ppt and after.ppt to experience the agony and the ecstasy for yourself...

I converted 33 brain-damaged bullet slides and made them all conform to a redesigned slide master in less than 10 minutes. I don't even want to think about how long it would have taken to have fixed them the conventional way. The only caveat is to watch for double-spaces and weird line breaks that Acrobat inserts. You'll want to go on a search-and-destroy mission for them.

And In the End...

In order to create Chapter 16, I asked several people open-ended questions about the ingredients that make up a successful presenter or presentation. My good friend Korie Pelka, who crafts them for a living, had the shortest and perhaps the most apt response.

"Knowledge and passion."

How perfect is that? Without them, not much else matters. With them, not much else is needed! To circle all the way back to where we started, this book cannot help you with that first ingredient: you have to know your stuff before you can put to use a single paragraph that we have written here.

Passion, on the other hand, can be found in many forms and the best presenters ensure that the audience feels their passion. It is the key to all that is good about designing and delivering presentations, and 267 pages later, it is our hope that we have fueled your passion for creating your next one.

Index

A

Adobe Illustrator, 78-79

Adobe Premiere, 114

Advanced Timeline, 45, 114

After Previous, 47-48, 95, 106-107, 143, 256

alpha channel, 78-79, 81-83

animation, 5, 12, 44, 49, 87, 93, 105, 144, 161, 166, 191, 193-195, 197-198, 200-201, 223, 228, 237, 248-249, 251, 255-256

B

background, 13-16, 33, 47, 52, 57, 63-64, 68, 72-75, 81, 85-86, 143, 148, 201, 215, 238, 263

bitmap, 72, 78, 80, 83-85, 247

blank the screen, 148

bullet slides, 4, 37-38, 43, 62, 265-267

C

Clipboard, 111, 174, 246

color scheme, 52, 54, 63, 125, 259-261

Context menu, 162

contrast, 17-18, 72-74, 127

Corel Corporation, 5

CorelDraw, 5, 30-31, 77-80, 83, 85, 110, 228, 231, 242, 247

custom show, 65-67, 69-70, 264-265

Customize, 163, 169-172, 223

D

Death by PowerPoint, 4, 88

design template
See template

digital camera, 194, 207, 213, 224

digital photography, 78, 84, 213

digital video, 226-227, 234, 241

dimming, 43, 49

dots per inch, 204

dpi
See dots per inch

E

Jim Endicott, viii, 1, 122-124, 153

EPS, 85

exit, 201

F

fade, 22-23, 33, 41, 44-46, 48, 68, 92-93, 100, 103, 108, 110, 112, 238, 251, 264

Flash, 90, 218, 227, 230, 241, 249

Formatting toolbar, 162

G

gestures, 122-128, 133, 136-137, 144

gradient, 47, 75-77, 261

H

handouts, 44, 59, 167

HTML, 170, 246, 248-249

hyperlink, 182-190, 194-199, 201-202, 229, 256, 265

I

inserted object, 189, 194, 196

L

laser pointer, 149

lectern, 127-128, 135, 140-141, 145, 147

M

macro security, 166

masters
    multiple master, 56

    slide master, 46, 51-55, 57-64, 68, 75, 91, 112, 171, 186-187, 196, 198, 201, 244, 257-258, 261, 263, 265-267

    title master, 54-55, 57, 61-62

Microsoft, 52, 161-162, 244-246, 250

motion path, 113-114, 116, 248

MP3, 235, 250

N

non-linear editing, 226

O

Object Linking and Embedding (OLE), 170, 189, 247

On Click, 42, 49, 92-93, 95, 191, 198, 200, 256

P

pan, 16, 208, 210, 226, 237, 254, 257, 260, 264

Paste Special, 174, 246-247

PDF, 85, 249, 265-266

PhotoPaint, 78-80, 208, 211, 213, 228, 238

Photoshop, 31, 78-80, 85, 194, 208, 211, 213, 228, 231, 242

pixel, 75, 78, 204-212

placeholder, 45, 48, 52-54, 57, 61-62, 75-76, 187, 198, 244-245, 261, 263, 265

PNG, 77, 79-83

.pot extension , 59-60, 67, 253

PowerPoint 2007, 56, 62-63, 84, 178, 226, 244, 258

PowerPoint Live, 11-12, 14, 33, 54-55, 67, 84, 88, 93, 106, 122, 176, 212, 226, 249, 259

PowerPoint Viewer, 199

Preserve Master, 258

R

Ribbon, 178, 245, 252

S

self-running presentations, 38, 59, 250-251

Slide Design, 57-60

slide masters
  See masters

Standard toolbar, 162, 173-174, 182, 193, 247

T

template, 52, 54-55, 57, 59-60, 63, 67, 70, 253, 257

Julie Terberg , 106, 125, 137

themes, 56, 63, 232

transition, 90-93, 112, 141-142, 230, 233, 236, 249, 251, 255-256, 264

transparency, 18, 71-79, 82-83, 108, 161, 201, 229, 231

V

Version 2007, 60-61, 83-84, 112, 178-179, 187, 244, 261

Viewer
  See PowerPoint Viewer

W

WAV, 165, 235, 237

wipe, 22, 33, 59, 92-93, 99, 103, 108, 251

With Previous, 45, 96, 102, 106-109, 115, 200, 256

X

XGA, 193, 205

Z

zoom, 23, 103, 116-117, 208, 210-211, 217, 226, 237